COMBAT KICK TECHNIQUES

COMBAT KICK TECHNIQUES

David Mitchell

LEOPARD

This edition published in 1996 by Leopard Books,
a division of Random House UK Limited,
20 Vauxhall Bridge Road, London SW1V 2SA

First published in 1989 by Stanley Paul

ISBN 0 7529 0214 8

Set in Linotron Plantin Light by Deltatype Ltd

Printed and bound in Great Britain by Scotprint, Musselburgh

Contents

Acknowledgements

I am delighted to acknowledge the substantial contributions made by the following to the writing of this book:

Ron Sergiew of the Taekwondo Association of Great Britain. Ron is a 5th Dan black belt and a British international. He has been training for 16 years and is based in the West Midlands. I asked Ron to contribute because I saw him compete with distinction at the World Championships in Oklahoma and believe that he is one of the finest exponents of kicking technique in the world.

Ron's assistant in the photos was Ellery James, a 1st Dan of the Taekwondo Association of Great Britain. Ellery is photographed on the receiving end of Ron's kicks.

Peter Spanton is the founder of the Higashi Karate Kai. He was one of Britain's first black belts and represented us on a number of occasions. His technique is so good that an 8th Dan world kata examiner once advised him to compete rather than to qualify as a kata judge. I asked Peter to contribute because I know that he has a wide knowledge of technique.

John Howard is a 3rd Dan black belt in Peter Spanton's Higashi Karate Kai. He kindly allowed himself to be on the receiving end of Peter's techniques and also demonstrated how not to perform certain techniques.

Martin Brierley teaches Wing Chun Kuen from his full-time Leeds training hall. He has been training for 14 years. I asked him to contribute, because whereas many teachers claim to be taught by Grandmaster Yip Man's son, I know for a fact that Martin actually does train under him. I therefore knew that whatever Martin demonstrated would be pure-line Wing Chun. I am indebted to him for revealing for the first time, in this book, the elegant sticking leg techniques of his style.

Stuart Palm acted as Martin's assistant. Stuart has been training for two and a half years and is a senior student in Martin's club.

The techniques I have described have been drawn not only from the above eminent contributors but also from those senior martial artists whom it has been my pleasure to know. Though the following did not contribute directly to this book, I thank them for the knowledge which they have passed on to me over the years:

Tommy Morris, for his lucid explanations of power development.

David 'Ticky' Donovan, for his in-depth analysis of karate technique.

I am not a medical expert, but it is my good fortune to be the son-in-law of the Chief Doctor to the World Union of Karatedo Organisations. Jim Canney has done more work on the identification of injury risk in training and injury prevention than any other doctor known to me, with the possible exception of the estimable Greg McLatchie. Jim has generously allowed me to quote liberally from his work.

Introduction

I well remember the first martial art competition I attended at London's Crystal Palace in 1965. One of the many participants knew how to perform a roundhouse kick to the head and when this fact became known to the audience, all eyes turned to watch his bouts. He was a leggy individual, with no hand techniques worth mentioning, yet he did have this devastating long-range kick and that alone took him through to the finals.

It wasn't that the kick was particularly good by today's standards; it was just so unexpected! Early martial artists got by in competition with the ubiquitous reverse-punch and the odd front kick, and since a high roundhouse kick was rarely encountered, they were simply not prepared for its range, or angle of delivery.

The efficacy of high kicks was by no means confined to the competition area. Early newspaper clippings confirmed that would-be muggers were floored by them too.

In my ignorance, I used to think that kicks could only be used effectively from middle-to-long distance but during the researching of this book, it soon became apparent that people with 'good legs' can stand a mere arm's length away and still deliver an effective high kick. At this point I do not want to debate the wisdom of kicking whilst in punching range; neither do I want to argue for or against the assertion that standing on one leg so close to the opponent is not a good thing! There is no doubt however, that the martial artist who can effectively use both hands and feet equally well, has a great advantage over the one who only knows how to use his fists.

Three factors are needed to acquire good kicking technique:

- constant practice, so the skill becomes 'grooved in',
- effective feedback, so mistakes can be corrected before they are grooved in,
- flexibility and power, so the kick can be performed safely to the required height and in the required direction, with the correct amount of force.

As a result of teaching martial art over a couple of decades or so, I have come to appreciate just how difficult kicking techniques can be for the average novice to learn. Most students could punch reasonably well within a short space of time but to reach an equivalent standard with kicks took significantly longer.

Since the arms and hands are used for a variety of purposes, they are more versatile and can be quickly applied to any new task. They are sufficiently strong, and their joints are flexible enough to perform complex techniques. By comparison, the legs are used for less varied functions and are less versatile. This is one of the reasons why leg techniques need more training time. Students who are also dancers or gymnasts learn kicking techniques more quickly than the average novice because they work their legs as much as their arms/hands.

Constant practice is only of real value when you can repeat techniques accurately and can concentrate on getting the form exactly right. If you tire fairly quickly, then the number of effective kick repetitions will fall and more sessions will be needed. Therefore you must develop enough of the right kind of fitness to sustain training. If your joints are sufficiently flexible, then you will be able to go for that extra few centimetres of height, confident that you will not pull a muscle. If your joints are free throughout their full range of movement, then your kick will accelerate smoothly at the correct angle to produce the most effective form.

Lack of flexibility in the hip joint is a major cause of poor kicks. Few novices can abduct or flex their hip joint sufficiently to produce an effective high kick. Attempting to kick high without the appropriate flexibility training is a waste of time. At best the student will learn a technique which is modified to make the required height; at worst, he will injure himself.

While working to improve flexibility, the student should content himself with aiming at a lower target. This will allow him to 'feel' the correct technique, and when flexibility is on tap, he will easily be able to lift the kick to the desired height.

Without doubt, getting yourself into a condi-

Few novices can abduct the hip joint sufficiently

Hip flexion may also prove a problem

tion where you can train effectively is as important as the training itself.

Being able to feel that a technique is correct is also important. At first novices don't know if they are doing something wrong so feedback can only come via the coach. The good coach can analyse and correct mistakes, putting the student into the correct position. When this is done often enough, the student learns to 'feel' the technique and thereafter needs less external correction. Top martial artists can tell solely by feel whether their technique is correct or not.

The good coach analyses and corrects mistakes, putting the student into the correct position

Once you understand the techniques, a mirror reflection or a videotape of your efforts will do much to help you spot the most obvious errors.

There are many schools of martial art and many ways of performing techniques. There is, however, no best martial art and no best way to perform a particular kick. There is only a best way for YOU personally. I have described the way kicks are performed in different schools but I have not compared one with another. It would be almost impossible to do so in a meaningful way.

Whichever school of martial art you follow, the principles of effectively using kicks are the same. These are:

- a clear target for the kick must be identified,
- the target must be brought into the correct range,
- the kick must be made at the right time, i.e., when the opponent isn't expecting it, and when he is moving in the correct direction,
- during its delivery, the kick must follow a path clear of the opponent's shoulders, elbows and knees,
- the kick must be delivered with sufficient power and control,
- the kick must be quickly retrieved after usage,
- balance must be maintained throughout.

Ultimately, the only measure of effectiveness is a personal one; if you regularly hit the target you aim for, with the required degree of force, then whatever you are doing, you are doing it correctly! Even so, there still may be avenues for slight improvement and hopefully this book will indicate them.

I don't want to give you the impression that this book is aimed solely at novices because it isn't! It is dedicated to ALL open-minded martial artists, regardless of grade or style, who want to develop effective kicking techniques to the highest possible standard.

David L. Mitchell
PENRITH
August 1988

1
Preparing to Practise

If you have to think about the kick you intend using, then your technique will simply be too slow. The only action that is fast enough is one in which the body takes over, and which is executed automatically. If you don't actually know a particular kick, then you won't be able to use it without conscious thought.

The first stage in learning any kick is to practise it in a series of stages, then to link those stages into a single flowing movement and, finally, to 'forget' the kick. You haven't actually forgotten it; what you have done is to learn it so well that when your mind snaps the command 'front kick', your body responds without hesitation.

If you find this difficult to understand, then think about driving a motor car. A learner driver finds difficulty in releasing the accelerator, disengaging the clutch and changing gear smoothly, whilst driving in the required direction. However, after a couple of lessons, he performs this complicated series of movements without thinking.

This acquisition of skill comes about through constant effective practice, but what do I mean by 'effective'? First of all you must perform sufficient repetitions of the kick within a set time, perhaps by the date of a certain grading examination. If you only practise your kick once a week over the usual 12-weekly inter-grading period, then by the time the grading comes around, you will only have practised it 12 times. Obviously this will not be enough to groove in the required level of skill, so you should actually repeat the kick many times during each training session.

'That's obvious!' I hear you say, but is it? Are you aware that skill acquisition is at its most effective when you are not fatigued? It is not possible to learn a new skill efficiently when you are collapsing from exhaustion. That is why new techniques must be learned either early on in the session, or by using muscles which have previously been resting. For example, you can practise kicks following a period of static punching activity.

The more times you repeat a kick without becoming fatigued, the quicker you will acquire the necessary level of skill. The kick involves an explosive burst of maximum speed both of the limb and of the whole body. Your kicks must acquire the correct distance and height, easily reaching the target you aim for. You must be able to kick from any position, quickly adapting to changing distances, and positioning yourself in the best place at any instant. You must be able to quickly work out what your opponent intends by reading his behaviour and responding in the shortest time with the appropriate technique. All this requires a certain mix of physical fitness factors, which I want to talk about before passing on to exercises and training proper.

Aerobic fitness arises out of the effectiveness of the lungs at taking in and absorbing oxygen from the air, the ability of the heart and blood vessels in transporting oxygen and food to the working muscles, the efficient usage of that oxygen by the muscles and the removal of waste products. It is the first system to be improved because it is the platform upon which all the other components of fitness rest. If you are aerobically fit, you can repeat a kick many times over at less than full power, without becoming fatigued.

To train aerobically involves raising your rate of heart beat into what is called the aerobic training band, and keeping it there for 15–20 minutes. The aerobic band lies between 70–75% of the maximum heart rate for healthy mature adults, i.e., between 120–140 beats per minute. However, if you are unfit, you may become tired after only 10 minutes or so. This isn't an insurmountable problem; it just means that you should begin training at a lower intensity, so you can last the full period.

The exercise used to achieve this depends upon what you like to do best. You can swim, cycle, jog, or use the appropriate system of weight training. Even better, you can practise the kicks themselves, though at less than maximum power. This last method has the added benefits of concurrently increasing mobility and improving skill. By regular committed training, you will find you can sustain more and more work. Within a comparatively short time, you will be ready to build on your aerobic fitness and go in for some really intensive work.

There is a level of training intensity at which the amount of oxygen supplied by the aerobic system is simply not enough to supply all the needs of the muscles. As this level is approached, there is a gradual shift in emphasis to an alternative energy supply system known as anaerobic respiration. The waste product of this system, lactic acid, builds up in the tissues, causing the muscles to reduce in efficiency and eventually stop working. Therefore the purpose of anaerobic training is:

i. to condition muscles to tolerate and function well despite high levels of lactic acid,
ii. to improve the reprocessing mechanisms which remove lactic acid.

Improvements in the type of anaerobic fitness which martial artists require come about through short duration/high intensity training. The level ultimately reached is determined by the relative distribution of the types of muscle fibres which a martial artist is born with. A good

Practise the kicks at less than maximum power to improve aerobic endurance

level of anaerobic fitness allows repeated powerful kicks.

As with aerobic fitness training, I prefer exercises which are most appropriate to the techniques to be improved. Therefore I recommend kicking against a pad, a kicking bag, or an airbag.

Deliver kicks with near-maximum power, one following the other without pause. When the muscles begin to fatigue, switch legs and repeat. Don't take a full rest because blood supply to the working muscles decreases within minutes, they stop pumping out waste products and the legs stiffen up.

Speed is the ability to move a limb and/or whole body quickly, and agility is being able to move about without fumbling or getting caught on the wrong foot. The martial artist must be able to kick quickly, giving little opportunity for the opponent to evade. Moreover he must kick equally well on either leg during fast stance changes, and whilst advancing or retreating. Agility can be improved by using the training drills which are suggested later in the book.

Strength is the effectiveness of a muscle or group of muscles in working against resistance. Despite its mass, the kicking leg must be accelerated and this requires a fair amount of strength. For our purposes, power is the muscle's ability to work quickly against resistance, so this is more important to martial artists than brute strength alone. Power generates impact force, so it is essential for an effective kick.

A point is reached when speed of muscle contraction cannot be increased. From there onwards, further gains in power can only be achieved through increases in strength. Fortunately muscles respond well to strength training and various drills are suggested later in the book.

Flexibility refers to the range of movement at a joint and so far as kicking techniques are concerned, the hip joint is the one which generally needs most flexibility training. A flexible hip allows the full range of kicks to be used and therefore confers a full measure of versatility. Maintaining a flexible hip is also a good safety measure because it allows a powerful kick to extend fully without tearing muscles. The opponent may be rather taller than you first estimated so this reserve of safety is a useful thing to have!

Increases in flexibility occur by stretching the muscles involved with, or acting through, the joint. Take care not to weaken the muscles; otherwise the joints will become unstable. Strength and flexibility training must always be combined for this reason.

I use the term 'mobility' to describe a range of smooth movement within the limits set by flexibility. General flexibility training involves taking the joint slowly to its limit and then extending it. This is quite different to dynamic mobility training. The latter ensures that a fast-moving kick reaches as high and as far as is intended. It is convenient at this point to mention something about safe training. The muscles operating the legs are powerful, and with a little training they can accelerate kicks to a very high speed. If nothing is done to check the

A flexible hip allows versatility and improves safety

kick, then the joints extend violently to their limits. If this happens once or twice, then probably no lasting harm is done, but if it is repeated many times, then there is a possibility that the joints and their associated tissues will suffer permanent damage.

The Chief Medical Officer of the Martial Arts Commission is convinced that repeated full power kicks against the empty air cause actual damage to the knee joint. He advises that such 'unloaded' kicks should only be performed slowly and that more powerful kicks be brought to a stop by an airbag, kicking bag, or impact pad.

From a skill point of view, kicking against the empty air develops techniques which work

The chief medical officer of the Martial Arts Commission believes that full power unloaded kicks may damage your joints

Bring powerful kicks to a stop using a punch bag or impact pad

against zero resistance. Although you may be unaware of it, subtle balance shifts and changes to body angles are necessary to permit powerful unloaded kicks. So if you only train this way, then the first time you try to kick hard at a resistance, you will not deliver your maximum potential impact.

Without wishing to be controversial, I would suggest that many black belts who perform beautiful looking unloaded kicks are in fact unable to kick a target effectively. Therefore from the points of view both of safety and of effectiveness, deliver powerful kicks only against a resistance.

Whilst on the topic of safety, let me give some more advice. Do not launch straight into hard

training. Warn your body what to expect by means of a proper warm-up and you will do much to reduce the possibility of injuries.

Training involves moving your legs in a different way and at a different speed to that to which they have been accustomed during the day. Warm-up prepares the body to face training, and by performing selected exercises, muscles and joints become freer and more flexible – so when you go for that extra inch of height in your side-kick, you won't pull a muscle!

As you get into the warm-up, your heart rate speeds up, increasing blood supply to working muscles. The muscles pump blood back to the heart and the body gradually readies itself for efficient training. Spend perhaps 10 minutes of a

90-minutes' training session on warm-up, finishing off with the first kicking techniques of training. Perform them with less than full power and gradually increase workload as the legs loosen up.

Warm-up is mental as well as physical. You must change mental gears as you move from a normal environment to a training situation. That which you do in the street may not be appropriate for the training hall, and vice versa. Therefore use warm-up to concentrate the mind on training, setting aside all worries and distractions.

Use warm-up also to help accurately locate the position of your arms and legs and the position of the body with regard to the floor. You may not be noticing an error in your technique simply because you are unaware that your arms and legs are in the wrong places!

Take what amounts to an active rest half way through the training session and perform specific flexibility exercises. By this time, muscles and

Poor flexibility may prevent you from abducting your hip sufficiently

It is better to kick low with good form, than high with bad form

joints will be operating at maximum efficiency and are able to respond effectively. This part of training is known as 'body preparation' and it extends the body's capabilities to meet the tasks imposed by kicking practice.

As I have already mentioned, kicking techniques require elements of flexibility etc., and if you don't possess these, then your kick will not be correct. You may wish to kick to the head but because of poor hip flexibility, you can't abduct your knee sufficiently. Either you accept this and temporarily lower your sights, or you adapt the technique so it appears to make the required height.

It is better to re-set your sights and perform the kick correctly to a lower height. Then you will learn the feel of a correct technique, and can apply this feel to the higher kick which you eventually achieve through body preparation. If, however, you adapt the technique, then you will learn the feel of an incorrect kick. It is then more difficult to unlearn it.

If you achieve success at a lower height, then you have something to fall back on if the subsequent and higher kick fails. Compare this with trying to kick high at the outset, and failing. Now there is no previous success to fall back on and the failure is therefore absolute. This can be demoralising and lead to a training block.

If you encounter such a block, then go around it rather than batter your head unsuccessfully against it. Who knows, if you achieve success in a related technique, you may become more confident and successfully re-tackle it. Avoid training blocks by setting targets which you believe you can reach within a reasonable time period. Don't compare yourself with others; set your own schedule and work to it. A measurable improvement in one's own performance builds enthusiasm, whereas comparing yourself to a more skilled classmate may produce despondency!

Some schools of martial art teach kicks in two quite different ways, the first being a basic form and the second being a more advanced variant. I don't know whether this is a good idea because it means having to learn two techniques instead of one. I appreciate that the basic form is easier to teach but would suggest that the advanced form is practised from day one, using feedback methods which help develop a correct feel.

As the training schedule proceeds, your body will adapt to the new requirements. This adaptation occurs during periods of rest, so allow for these in your programme. Do remember that all training is reversible. This means quite simply that if you don't maintain a constant programme of training, you will very soon slip back to your original level of fitness.

In conclusion, a cool-down is as important as the warm-up. The muscles have been pumping away and are full of fluids and waste products. If you stop abruptly, these will be stranded in the muscles, causing aches and pains. Go on performing kicks but at a slowing pace for a short while after training proper finishes, then do some gentle muscle contracting and stretching exercises.

2
Training Aids

A number of training aids are available to help you to develop effective kicks. For example, a mirror shows what you are actually doing, rather than what you think you might be doing. Training in front of a mirror is done at your own pace and you can cover the topics you feel you need, when you want.

Training aids which allow impact are useful for testing that you have:

- formed your foot correctly so it can withstand heavy contact without flexing painfully at the ankle, or hurting the toes,
- aligned the foot correctly, so it strikes effectively with the correct part,
- set your stance up correctly, so you aren't knocked off balance by recoil,
- delivered the technique so it actually digs into the target, and doesn't glance off,
- delivered the technique so it literally 'explodes' on the target.

The impact pad is an excellent training aid because it allows you to kick a target which has the same mass as an opponent. The best pads are made from layers of stiff, closed-cell plastic foam sandwiching a softer, central layer. The various layers are welded together so they can't separate and the whole is enclosed in a slick plastic case.

The pad is held either against the chest or more generally against the upper arm. The upper arm position is better for receiving powerful kicks. The kick is made into the centre of the pad and your partner prepares for impact by leaning into the kick and tensing at the moment of impact.

The pad must be presented square-on, other-wise the kick may skid off and perhaps strike your partner. Most pads are fairly small, so accuracy is very important – especially with reverse-turning kicks! I always remember a particular turning kick to the stomach missing its target, and fetching the partner a resounding clout in the groin! Larger impact pads can be obtained, though these suffer from their own disadvantages in use.

An impact pad provides a target with the same mass as an opponent

Kick the target mitt with a variety of techniques

Don't be surprised if you fall over the first time you kick the pad. The martial artist trained exclusively on a diet of unloaded kicks will find that recoil affects stability. Kick slowly at first, gradually building up speed as you become more confident. The object of training is to develop a fast and focused impact that produces a sharp shockwave rather than a powerful push.

When you can kick the pad quickly and effectively with a variety of techniques, then learn how to range on a moving target. The partner moves suddenly forwards, or away from you, and there is only a split second to respond. Stop-kick the pad as it advances, or step back sharply and kick if distance is too short for an effective focus of power. Chase the pad as it moves away, closing distance sufficiently to kick it powerfully.

Target mitts are gloves faced with thick padding. They are excellent for speed and accuracy training, but are not so useful for power training. Front-kicks, side-kicks and back-kicks all tend to slide off and can sprain your partner's wrist in the process. Mitts are well-suited for training in non-contact types of competition.

Your partner holds the mitts up as you run through your syllabus of kicks. Next, he holds one mitt down against his thigh, swinging it up to present either the face or side. You must respond quickly and accurately with a suitable kick.

Next your partner moves around, obliging you to kick a moving target presented at different heights. The mitts are moved up and down, and from side to side. They are held apart to encourage fast attacks on widely separated targets. Once presented, the mitt is left out until your technique connects with it. Any openings in your guard can be painlessly pointed out with the mitts.

The airbag is a light, inflatable pad with loops through which an arm can be inserted. It is both easy and comfortable to use and causes little damage to the feet even over long periods of practice. It is, however, difficult to use with straight kicks – they tend to glance off as the bag swivels on its arm loops.

A punching bag is a useful training aid for most kicks but begin with light impacts before increasing to full force. Some bags are quite heavy! They are best filled with polystyrene granules or rags, though some masochists have been known to use sawdust, or even sand! You should be able to hit the bag repeatedly with full force, without jarring your joints or bruising the contact areas.

Aim for sharp impacts rather than shoves which make the bag swing wildly. If it does start swinging, ask your partner to hold it steady. Punching bags are probably the best all-round impact training aid, though they take up a lot of room.

The wooden man dummy is a traditional training aid for Chinese martial arts of the Shaolin tradition. It consists of a baulk of timber, with short spars projecting at odd angles. The whole thing is suspended on springy laths which in turn are fixed to a supporting frame. The timber baulk represents the body, the spars the arms and legs. The angle and

Kicks are delivered on the move, as you step from one side of the wooden dummy to the other

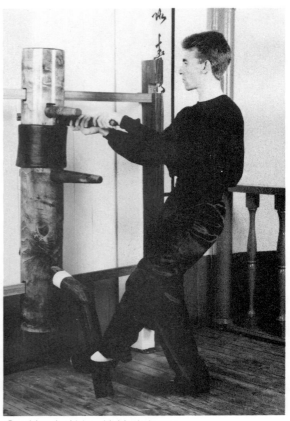

Combine the kicks with blocks/grasps

height of the spars are set up as per traditional measurements but as a concession to today's martial artist, parts of the timber baulk are wrapped with impact absorbent material.

The spars make one aware that the opponent is not a simple smooth tube, such as a punching bag. Instead he is all angles, elbows and knees, which must be avoided. The wooden man has an equivalent weight to an opponent, so it responds to correct impacts. Kicks are delivered on the move, shifting from one side of the dummy to the other. The spars are treated as the opponent's potential hand techniques so most kicks are accompanied by blocks or grasps.

The wooden man dummy is well adapted to those Chinese schools which train with it, but I would advise students of other traditions to use it only with the greatest care.

3
Developing Power

The object of power training is to develop impact force to the maximum which you can realistically achieve, having regard to your size and build. Obviously, the bigger you are, the greater potential you have for generating force. Smaller people are obliged to make good any deficit in their muscles by relying upon improvements in accuracy, distancing, timing, and evasion.

Some martial artists inject every ounce of power and determination into the conclusion of a powerful kick, tensing all muscles for an instant of time. As the diaphragm (the muscle band below the ribs responsible for breathing) tightens, air is driven out of the lungs, producing a staccato grunt. This is sometimes vocalised into a short, explosive 'EEE!' It is low-pitched and quite unlike the shriek produced from the upper chest by the tightening of the intercostal muscles.

Various claims have been made about the power developed by this shout but it may well be no more than a side-effect of muscle spasm.

The commitment of all the body's energies into a single kick (which may after all, miss and take time to recover) may, in any case, not be a good idea.

Be that as it may, the body is certainly capable of absorbing a great deal of impact when it is tightened by muscular spasm.

One suggestion for developing power is to throw the foot at the target in a relaxed manner, only tightening up as it is about to land and then localising the contraction in the foot alone. It is certainly difficult to kick at maximum speed when the limb you are using is tensed, so relax muscles which are not involved in generating the movement.

The national coach of the British Karate Federation team always advises his students to perform front kick with the heel carried slightly low and toes relaxed but not pulled back. Because of the foot angle, the toes flex back

One-step kicks are powerful because the step forward acts as an accelerator

naturally on impact. This is good advice because pulling back the toes uses a muscular contraction which stiffens much of the lower leg and slows the kick.

Any kick can be made more powerful if you move body weight behind it. A forwards shift of body weight over just a couple of inches is sufficient to generate a force called 'momentum'. Momentum is a property of moving bodies and it yields a substantial bonus in impact energy. It also soaks up the recoil of impact; a useful concomitant if you are a small person.

The faster the body moves, the greater the momentum generated. One-step kicks are powerful because the step acts as an accelerator. One drawback however, is the rather obvious cue this gives to the opponent. A good compromise is a drag forwards of the supporting leg behind the kick. Though this movement may only be over a couple of centimetres, it is sufficient to generate

Step both in front and behind the supporting leg

Turning your hips into a kick makes it more powerful

momentum energy. A lot of practice is needed to synchronise the drag forwards with the moment of impact and if forward movement stops before the kick lands, then momentum is shed before it can be used.

The pelvic girdle is situated near the body's centre of gravity and techniques delivered through it are less susceptible to recoil. Turning your hips behind a kick brings more than just the muscle power of your legs into play.

Plyometrics is an aspect of modern power training which has long been recognised by martial artists. The principle behind it is that a stretched muscle is loaded with additional energy, and this can be simply shown by dropping down into a half squat. Jump as high as you can in the air and measure the height you reached. Then bob down from a standing position into the half squat immediately before jumping. This time you will jump higher, because you pre-stretched the responsible muscles and loaded them with energy.

This is the principle used in 'skip-stepping' before a kick. In some schools, the hips are driven forwards during a front kick, so the stomach muscles are stretched. The lower leg lags behind the rapidly rising knee, so the muscles on the front of the thigh are also stretched. When the lower leg is driven out, these pre-stretched muscles contract with greater power.

Similarly for the roundhouse kick, the upper body both rotates and leans away, stretching the muscles of the side and back. This gives additional power to the kick.

There are two schools of thought on how the lower leg is thrust out. One says that it is

The upper body both rotates and leans away during roundhouse kick

passively snapped forwards – as though cracking a whip. The other recommends powering the foot all the way to the target. Bearing in mind the importance of a fast kick, try both methods out on a kicking bag or impact pad and judge for yourself which generates the most force.

Whichever you choose, always withdraw your foot promptly afterwards, so it cannot be caught by the opponent.

4

Fitness Training

This is a selection of exercises, which I have found to be effective. The selection is neither total nor exclusive, and you may well come across others which you think are better. If you do so, then by all means use them!

Many of the exercises selected may be practised alone, but a few which require a partner are also included. Exercise at a steady rate and don't overdo things – especially at first. Don't just train in the training hall, practise at home too.

Begin with a general warm-up and run through a programme of mobility exercises, starting from the neck and working down through the joints, finishing at the ankles. A methodical approach ensures that you miss nothing. Pick those exercises which you feel work best for you.

My selection contains a preponderance of leg-stretching and mobility exercises. This is because:

- the training session which follows is exclusively intended for leg-work,
- the shoulder is generally flexible enough for most techniques, whereas the hip seldom is.

Warm-up Exercises

Begin the warm-up gently and gradually increase the level of activity. Remember that the object is to loosen yourself up – not tire yourself out – before skill acquisition can begin.

Run on the spot, raising knees high and pumping your arms. Skip without using a rope and kick your heels up. Jump up and down, making each tenth jump higher than the rest. Pull your knees to your chest. Then twist around as you jump, measuring off quarter and half turns. This teaches you how to position yourself during flying kicks. Jump high and land with legs and arms splayed wide; then jump again, bringing arms to sides and feet together. Set a regular rhythm for these splay jumps.

Turn your head from side to side, smoothly and without force. Tilt your head back and look upwards; pause, then lower it onto your chest. Rock your head from side to side, and then roll it

Jump high and pull your knees up

Twist around as you jump, measuring off quarter- and half-turns

Circle your arms in the same direction, then in opposite directions

in a full circle, first one way, then the other. This latter exercise can cause dizziness.

Bend forwards at the waist and swing your arms backwards and forwards allowing them to bend naturally at the elbows. Gradually speed up, keeping both arms relaxed. Straighten your arms and circle them in the same direction, then in opposite directions. After 30 seconds or so of this, bend your elbow and raise one arm to the side of your head. Grasp your elbow in the other hand and gently pull it back. Repeat the exercise a number of times and then change arms. Alternatively, link your fingers behind the back

of your neck. If you can't manage this, use a belt to bridge the gap and 'walk' your fingers towards each other.

Work your wrist joints through their full range of movement and shake them vigorously. Put the palms of your hands together, as though in prayer, and draw the forearms downwards. Then put the backs of your hands together and lower the forearms.

Stand with feet well separated and both arms extended above your head. Bring the backs of your hands together and interlace the fingers. Lean first to one side, then to the other, always

Lean first one way, then the other   Twist your upper body

pushing your arms out as far as they will go. There are other ways of doing this particular exercise, but I happen to consider that this is the most effective. Bring your arms down and twist your upper body as though to look behind. Hold the twisted position briefly and then relax from it.

Go into press-up position and bend your elbows, allowing your body to drop down and forward. Then fully extend the elbows, dropping the hips to the floor and arching the back. Move backwards to the start position and repeat the exercise.

Bend forward and touch the floor in front of your feet. Your knees point straight ahead and your feet are slightly parted. Keep your arms straight and allow upper body weight to increase spine flexion. Spend at least ten seconds at the point of greatest stretch. Then straighten up and lean back as far as possible into what is called 'a

back hyper-extension'. Alternatively, bend your knees and place the palms of your hands flat on the floor. Then gradually straighten your knees while keeping the palms flat. A more strenuous version begins from press-up position. Walk forwards, keeping your hands flat on the floor, until your toes come to a stop behind your wrists and your knees are fully extended. Then return to press-up position by stepping backwards.

Finally, bend forward and roll your upper body in a wide circle while reaching out with both arms. Repeat trunk circling in the opposite direction.

Extend one leg and lower bodyweight over the other by bending the knee. Brace your upper body with your arms, keeping both feet flat on the floor. Increase stretch by bending the supporting knee still further. Maintain balance by leaning forwards between your knees. Do not bounce on the extended leg because rather than

Go into press-up position

Flex your elbows

Lower your body down

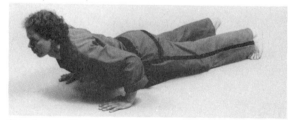

Skim forward between your arms

Drop your hips to the floor and arch your back

Bend forward and touch the floor. Keep your knees straight

Extend one leg and lower your weight over the other.
Don't bounce down

increasing flexibility, this may actually cause damage. Repeat the exercise equally on both sides.

Turn your hips so they face in the direction of your leading foot. Then bend the front knee, allowing the heel of your rear foot to rise, but keeping your rear leg as straight as possible. This stretches the muscles on the front and inside of your extended leg. Extend the forward stance still further whilst keeping your body upright. Drop the rear knee to the floor.

Turn your hips and drop your rear knee to the floor

Extend your legs in front and behind

Extend your legs in front and behind, working them as far out as they will go. Take some of the weight on the tips of your fingers. Leg extension is gradual and jerking or bouncing actions must be avoided. Hold lowest position for at least ten seconds. Repeat the exercise on the other side. Then turn your hips forwards and perform box splits. Don't support yourself by pressing on your knees with your hands.

Go into up press-up position and bend your knees, lowering them to the floor and opening them as wide as possible. Move your weight

Lower and open your knees. Move your weight backward and forward

forwards, stretching the muscles on the insides of the thighs. Then return to the starting position and repeat the exercise. Unlike box splits, this puts no lateral pressure on the knee joints – and this is a good thing if you suffer from knee problems.

Sit down and extend both legs in front of you, keeping the backs of your knees pressed firmly to the floor. Lean forwards and extend your arms, holding greatest stretch for at least ten seconds. The weight of the arms gradually draws down the upper body and improves the stretch. Repeat this a number of times and then open your legs wide. Take hold of your heels and draw your chest down to the floor. Even better, extend both

Lean forward, pulling your chest to your knees

Lean forward between your splayed legs

arms between your open legs as far as they will go. Hold lowest position for a minimum count of ten seconds, then switch to a side-to-side movement, sweeping both arms from one ankle to the other. Stretch forwards at the same time.

Roll forwards onto your hands whilst keeping the legs open and stretched. Arch your back and look upwards.

Lever your knees out and push them down

Suppport yourself on your hands and arch your back

Pull your rear foot back and lower your head onto the leading knee

Sit back and extend one leg. Draw the other up to the inside of your thigh and bend forwards until your forehead touches the extended knee. Hold lowest position for at least ten seconds. Change legs and repeat the exercise. Then withdraw the bent leg, bringing the foot to your backside. Try to get a right-angle bend between your upper legs. Begin as before, lowering your head to the leading knee; then straighten up before lowering your head towards the flexed knee. Hold lowest position. Finally drop your head to the floor, midway between the knees. Change legs and repeat the exercise.

Cross one leg over the other and lever your hips over

Bring both feet in and bend the knees, so the soles are pressed together. Put your elbows inside your knees, levering them outwards and downwards. Hold the lowest position for at least ten seconds, then relax and repeat the exercise. Cross one leg over the other and use your shoulder to lever your upper leg over.

Roll onto your back, lifting both feet over your head. Brace yourself by extending your arms to either side. Keep both knees straight, supporting yourself on shoulders and balls of feet. Open your legs out wide. Then roll onto your lower back, grasping your ankles without bending the knees. Pull your feet towards you and outwards.

Roll onto your back and straighten the knees

Open your legs wide

Lie on your back and wriggle so your backside comes to press against a wall. Extend your legs and allow them to separate under their own

Allow your legs to abduct under their own weight

weight. When the stretch becomes uncomfortable, lift them slightly and hold for at least ten seconds. Relax them once more. Though this exercise may appear rather easy, it is not! It is a particularly forceful stretch made all the more effective by the gradual effect of gravity.

Put your hands on your waist and circle your hips, first one way, then the other. Lift your knee and rotate your leg in a wide circle, first in one direction, then in the other. Perform this exercise equally on both legs.

Put your hands on your hips and circle your hips

Flex your knee… then circle your hip joint   Swing your leg forward and up…and to the side

Take up a long stance and swing your back leg forward and up. Because of the risk of muscle injury, the leg must not be swung violently. Repeat the leg swing ten times and change to the other leg. Stand facing a support and cross your right foot in front of the left. Grasp the support and swing your right foot up and outwards in a sideways arc. Do not swing too hard. The effect of this exercise is reduced if, during the swing, you let the ball of the foot rise higher than the heel. Repeat ten times and change legs. Hold the support and swing your leg up and backwards. Keep the knee straight – don't let it hook upwards.

Leg swings such as these are mobility exercises, moving the hip joint between limits set by flexibility. Do not mistake this for flexibility training, which it is not!

Lift a foot up and behind, so you can grasp the ankle. Pull the foot upwards into the small of your back. Then bend the knee as far as possible and pull the sole of your foot tight into your backside. Drop into a kneeling position and sit

with feet extended. Keep your back upright and sit on your heels, then increase stretch by leaning backwards.

Face a wall in a long forward stance. Reach forwards with both arms and push against it, keeping both feet flat on the floor. Don't bend the rear knee. Hold position for ten seconds and then raise the heel for a further ten seconds. Drop the heel once more. Alternatively stand on

a step and drop your heel below it. Raise the heel so you come to tiptoe and then drop it back again.

Return to a sitting position and extend one leg. Cross the other over it and grasp your ankle. Use your other hand to rotate the foot, first one way, then the other.

Improving Aerobic Endurance

As I mentioned earlier, kicking techniques cannot be learned efficiently if fatigue prevents you from repeating them enough times. The first stage in staving off fatigue is to increase your level of aerobic fitness. The programme for achieving this can be tailored to suit your present condition and as long as it raises your heart beat into the training band, the desired result will be obtained. If you are unfit, then aim for the lower reaches of the band and gradually increase training pace as your fitness level improves.

As your aerobic fitness level rises, increase your heart rate with harder training, until it reaches the top of the band. Then reduce exercise intensity so the heart rate drops to the lower limit. Keep raising and lowering the heart rate throughout the session.

If you want to check your heart rate, gently press two fingers into the side of your neck near the windpipe. Count for six seconds and if you record less than 14 beats, increase the pace of training. If you count more than 14, then slow down because you are entering the anaerobic band and this will not help your aerobic fitness. The figures I have given are appropriate to an aerobically fit martial artist. You may need to reduce the heart rate in order to last the full session.

If you have access to gymnasium facilities, then use a cycling or rowing machine, or a power jogger. Variety is the spice of life, so use each piece of apparatus on different days. Gymnasium training is an easy option, because it is sheltered from the elements.

Sophisticated equipment always includes some form of effort measurement and I strongly advise you to keep a record of the results. Don't go at it too hard and sessions will soon show a steady improvement.

Weight training is an interesting way to increase aerobic capability. Raise your heart rate into the training band by selecting weights which are about 40% of what you can manage to lift in one go. Set out a circuit of different exercises, doing 20/30 repetitions of each before moving to the next.

If you prefer outdoor training, then choose swimming, cycling, or cross country running. Running on hard roads is not recommended because of the hammering it gives the legs and spine. Overweight martial artists in particular may find that jogging does not help the back. Cycling is a good way to train and it does not damage the knees.

Use alternative legs to kick repeatedly a suspended bag, maintaining a rhythm and changing both kick height and type. Repeat-kick on the same leg and sometimes skip-jump between steps, so you are constantly working. Do not kick hard.

Improving Anaerobic Endurance

If you train too hard, your heart rate will increase beyong the upper limit of the aerobic training band and fatigue will build up as excess lactic acid is produced. If you are using one group of muscles more than others, then these will tire first. Anaerobic training builds on the platform you have gained through your aerobic programme. The higher that platform, the longer fatigue is staved off.

The exercise which you select must be appropriate but otherwise it is simply a case of performing as many repetitions as you can within one minute, rather than doing the maximum number of repetitions for any particular exercise. Take active rest periods between sets of repetitions.

Squats are excellent for training leg muscles, so aim to do up to a hundred. Begin from feet apart position, dropping into a half squat with thighs parallel to the floor and knees pointing outwards above the toes. Straighten up quickly. Don't drop into a full squat and bounce back up because this can damage knee joints.

Martial artists with powerful leg muscles can perform squats with a weight across the shoulders. Don't use heavy weights because we are looking for speed as well as strength of contraction. Rest the weight bar across the shoulders and behind your neck. Keep your back straight, turn your feet slightly outwards and open your knees. Lower yourself into a half squat position and then thrust strongly upwards. Vary the training effect by holding the bar across the front of your chest.

Beware the effects of momentum when performing squats with weights. Do not drop below a half squat, and do allow the weight to come to rest before extending the knees.

A further alternative is to drop into a half squat position and as the knees extend, raise one leg and perform a high front kick. Repeat this on each leg alternately for around 30/50 repetitions. Better still, work at maximum speed and see how many repetitions you can do within 60 seconds.

Use two benches, one on top of the other – or a high step of some kind. Raise one knee and step onto the platform. Straighten your leg, raising your body up so the other foot can be put down alongside the first. Step down with the first leg, following it with the other. Count the number of completed step-ups you can achieve within 60 seconds. Spring onto the platform to get the best training effect. Stronger martial artists can repeat this exercise with a light weight across their shoulders.

Use a time limit also to see how many full-power kicks of different types you can put into a bag. Kick equally on both legs. Repeat the exercise after a short, active rest period.

When you are reasonably pleased with your anaerobic performance and can kick repeatedly hard and fast, try short (no more than 15 seconds) explosive attacks on the bag. This regime is useful for training that part of the anaerobic energy supply known as 'the phosphagen system'. A long rest period is needed before the exercise can be meaningfully repeated.

Strength Training

Many strength training exercises are to be found in the section dealing with anaerobic performance. Squats, squat-kicks and step-ups not only

improve endurance, but benefit strength as well. Strength training loads the muscles as they work, so adaptive changes take place. Pumping heavy weights will tend to develop a slow-moving strength which, I suggest, is not what we are looking for. Aim instead to move lighter weights quickly. If you don't have access to weights, then use body weight.

Kicking movements use not only the muscles of the leg, but those of the body also. A general whole-body strength training programme is therefore no bad thing for the martial artist who wants to improve his kicks.

Begin with the shoulders and upper body. Drop into press-ups position, with the back straight and your elbows flexed. Support yourself on the balls of your feet and the flats of your hands, fingertips, or knuckles. Lower

Take up the press-up position and lower yourself down until your chest touches the floor

Vary the training effect by turning your hands inward

yourself until your chest touches the floor; pause, then extend your elbows until they lock straight. Repeat the exercise at least 25 times, aiming eventually at 100 repetitions. Vary the training effect by turning your hands in towards each other.

Increase load by resting your feet on a bench and pressing-up. Practise explosive movement by dropping into full elbow flexion and thrusting up powerfully, so your feet and hands clear the floor.

your torso from side to side as you sit up. When you can perform 100 sit-ups, cuddle a weight to your chest and repeat the exercise. Alternatively, use an inclined surface to do a sit-up against gravity.

Lift both knees to meet your shoulders

Thrust up clear of the floor to develop explosive strength in the upper body

Lift your knee to meet your raised shoulders

Sit-ups strengthen the stomach muscles. Flex your knees and lift your shoulders clear of the floor; pause, and then lower them back again. Improve your roundhouse kick by swivelling

Lift extended legs and lean forward to touch your toes

Knee lifts are excellent for improving hip flexion. Lie back and bring one knee up. Lift your shoulders off the floor to meet it. Vary the training effect by bringing both knees back to your chest. Lift extended legs in a vee-sit, reaching forward with your arms to touch them.

Use a partner to provide resistance to specific kicking movements. Stand in fighting stance, with a belt tied securely around your rear ankle. Your partner holds the other end of the belt. He resists as you lift your knee up and forwards for a front kick. A few kicks are sufficient for both partners to adjust to the exercise.

The leg must be allowed to move without too much resistance, otherwise the kicking technique will undergo an unwelcome modification. Allow the leg a relatively free initial movement, thereafter steadily increasing resistance as the knee rises. Elastic bungee straps will provide a similar training effect if a partner is unavailable.

Single-leg bounds develop plyometric power

Plyometric Training

Plyometric training develops explosive power in the leg muscles. The principle is that muscles must be pre-stretched in the instant before they contract. The sharper the pre-stretch, the greater the plyometric effect.

Perhaps the most obvious plyometric exercise is squat-jumps, where you bob down and spring into the air. If your knees are up to it, jump down from a platform and land on the balls of your feet. Bend your knees and spring onto a facing platform. Turn around and repeat the exercise. Perform several repetitions and then have an active rest before repeating the sequence.

Single-legged bounds from side to side develop the legs separately and prevent the stronger leg from taking an unfair share of work. Always land on the balls of the feet and spring quickly up again.

Flexibility Training

Flexibility training extends the range of movement at a joint by stretching the muscles associated with it. Ultimately, the degree of flexibility is limited by the bony structures of the joint, but in most people an earlier flexibility limit is imposed by strong muscles. These muscles must first be relaxed before they can be stretched effectively. The warm-up is effective for this, as is aerobic training or strength/endurance work.

The muscle is equipped with a stretch sensor which protects it from movements likely to cause damage, and a gradually increasing stretch is less likely to cause a reflex muscle contraction than a jerky movement. Do not apply too much force, or the muscle may be damaged. Stop at the point of discomfort.

Most flexibility work for kicks involves stretching the muscles in the inside of the thighs (the 'thigh adductors'), and on the backs of the thighs (the 'hamstrings').

Many of the stretching exercises performed during warm-up can be improved through the assistance of a partner. The first which springs to mind is that seated exercise in which both legs are extended. Gentle pressure against the back will help stretch the relaxed muscles.

Lean forward and touch your forehead to the extended kneecap

Stand sideways-on to your partner

Put your foot on your partner's shoulder and extend your knee. Your partner slowly straightens up, lifting your leg higher until you signal for a stop. Hold the highest position for a count of ten. Keep the supporting foot flat on the floor and draw your shoulders to the extended knee.

Stand sideways-on and straighten your leg, hooking the toes around the back of your partner's neck. If your hips aren't very flexible, ask him to stoop, or even drop onto one knee. He then gradually stands up. Grasp the underside of your knee and pull your head forwards. Keep the same position but lower your chest to the knee of the supporting leg.

Raise your knee to the side, as though performing a roundhouse kick. The partner takes your raised knee on top of his shoulder and holds it there. Tell him to stop when the point of actual discomfort is reached. There is nothing to gain by being brave.

When maximum stretch is reached, extend the raised knee and point your toes. Always keep the supporting foot flat on the floor and don't allow the heel to rise. Twist your upper body away.

When you have acquired a fair degree of flexibility, try a more advanced system known as 'PNF'. This works by fooling the muscle sensors into allowing more stretch. To illustrate how this works, I have chosen an exercise we have already done. Sit down and gather your legs in close, with soles of feet pressed together. Grasp your ankles. Your partner applies firm pressure down onto the knees so the muscles on the inside of the thighs are stretched. Hold greatest stretch for ten seconds and then contract your thigh adductors, forcing the knees up against the pushing force. Hold contraction for ten seconds and then relax once more.

Your partner presses down for 30 seconds

Lower your chin to the knee of the supporting leg

Your partner lifts the flexed knee

The partner presses down on your knees

before releasing. Repeat the process two or three times. The muscles will stretch a little more following contraction.

As a second example, lie on your back and lift a straight leg into the air. Your partner grasps your foot and pushes it back towards your shoulders. Hold maximum stretch, then try to force your leg against the applied pressure. After ten seconds contraction, relax and allow the leg to be stretched further.

Stretch the hamstrings using the PNF method

Also use PNF to stretch the thigh adductor muscles

Agility

Train for agility with short sprints that incorporate sudden changes in direction of at least 90°. Bound from side to side in a series of one-legged leaps and repeatedly jump/switch stance from left to right in quick succession.

Skip from left to right stance and as you land, immediately kick with the rear leg. Skip quickly – not high.

5
Front Kick

General Features of Kick

Front kick either thrusts the ball of the foot deeply into the opponent, or it delivers a sharp 'dig' to a vulnerable part of the opponent's body. There are various types of front kick, all of which use the muscles of the upper leg and lower torso to accelerate the knee to a position where the kick can be effectively delivered.

As a general principle, as little warning as possible is given to the opponent. The kicking knee is quickly raised and brought forward so it covers your lower stomach. The foot travels in the most direct way to the target and is retrieved with equal speed afterwards. Momentum must be controlled, otherwise the body will lurch forward as the kick extends.

Part of Foot Used

Orthodox front kick strikes with the ball of the foot. This is an effective weapon, combining padding over vulnerable bones with a narrow impact zone to concentrate force efficiently. The toes are pulled back to protect them from injury either by muscular action or by relaxing them so they flex back naturally upon impact. Valuable speed may be lost if you use excessive and premature muscular action to form the correct foot-shape.

The instep is in line with the shin. Practise the correct foot-shape by lifting your heel as far off the ground as possible, whilst pressing the ball of the foot firmly down.

Thrusting Kick to Midsection

Begin from fighting stance by first changing your guard and twisting on your supporting leg, so

Front kick thrusts the ball of the foot deeply into the opponent

The toes are pulled back and the instep is virtually in line with the shin. The heel is slightly lowered

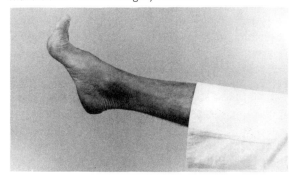

The kicking knee is quickly raised and brought forward to cover the lower stomach

Begin from fighting stance. Novices may find it easier to change guard at this point

The foot travels in the most direct way to the target

Thrust out the lower leg into the projected midline of your own body

the rear hip is brought forward. As this happens, raise your rear leg and lift the sole of the foot directly off the floor. Springing up with the heel may well provide a faster start to the kick though it is then more difficult actually to thrust the foot out.

Avoid inadvertently opening your groin to attack as your knee raises. Brush the supporting leg with the ankle of your kicking foot, raising the knee until it points at the target. The supporting knee is slightly bent and the foot twists outwards to a 90° angle. Keep your elbows to your sides so your arms don't flap about. Relax your shoulders and they won't give a telltale shrug.

As your knee reaches the correct height, thrust out the lower leg directly into the projected midline of your own body. The movement of the lower leg must merge with the action of the rising knee, otherwise the kick becomes jerky and power is wasted.

Lift the sole of your foot directly off the floor

Raise the knee until it points at the target

Keep your elbows to your sides and don't let them flap about

Pull your foot back smartly after impact

The object is to thrust your foot forward rather than swing it upwards. If it skids up the front of the target, then you haven't used your hips correctly. Project your hips forward and lean back slightly to keep your head above the supporting foot.

Pull your foot back smartly after impact and set it down. If you have kept your weight over the supporting leg, then it will be easy to place the foot carefully. Provided you changed guard at the outset, you will land with an effective posture.

Faults to Watch Out For

The faults commonly encountered in front kick are listed below, together with the remedies for dealing with them:

Weight is biased over the kicking leg so a body shift is first needed to allow the leg to be used. This warns the opponent.	Use a stance with a neutral weight bias, or one with weight biased over the non-kicking leg.
The guard is not changed during an advancing front kick, so you land in an open posture.	Change guard hands over during kick. Novices will find it easier to change guard before the kick gets under way.

Novices should change guard…   …before kicking

The kick appears jerky.	Keep shoulders relaxed, especially when changing guard.
The elbows 'flap' during the kick.	Keep shoulders relaxed. Let the arms hang naturally and hold the elbows lightly to your sides.
The heel of the kicking foot lifts before the sole, making it difficult to thrust the foot out in the correct way.	Practise pulling your foot into the air, so the sole and heel stay parallel to the floor.

If the heel lifts before the toes, the inexperienced student will find it difficult to thrust the foot forwards in the correct configuration

The kicking knee does not rise high enough, so the final kick is too low.	Stretch the hip flexors using the exercises given in the chapter on fitness. Use a chair to train knee lift.
The groin opens as the knee rises.	Bring the kicking foot close by the supporting knee.

The kicking action is jerky because the lower leg is thrust out after the knee has finished lifting.	Synchronise the kicking action so the lower leg begins to thrust out before the knee has finished lifting.
The kicking foot swings upwards past the target instead of thrusting into it.	Turn the hips behind the kick and/or thrust the lower leg out before the knee has finished lifting.
The body leans backwards, so the head lies behind the supporting heel. This reduces ability to cope with recoil.	Lean back only so the back of the head is directly above the heel of the supporting leg.

Leaning back too far makes the kick unstable

The martial artist appears to bob up and down during a series of front kicks.	Keep the supporting leg bent during the kick.
The toes are not pulled back far enough, or are too stiff to flex sufficiently and are stubbed on impact.	Practise the correct foot configuration by ressing down on the floor with the ball of the foot and lifting the heel.
The foot is not extended, so impact is made with the sole.	Increase flexibility of the ankle joint and practise correct foot configuration as above.

The body falls forward as the kick is retrieved, the foot slapping down hard on the floor.

Control over the body's centre of gravity has been lost. Weight must be concentrated over the supporting foot.

Training Aids

Use a mirror to check that:

- you are keeping your groin closed during the kick,
- you are kicking to the centre,
- you are not leaning too far back during kick extension,
- your shoulders are not hunching up as you raise your knee,
- your elbows do not rise away from your sides.

Use a punch-bag to check that:

- your foot is configured correctly,
- your kick is striking into the bag and not skating up it,
- you are generating impact force,
- you are able to resist the effects of recoil.

Use a chair to encourage you to raise your foot high enough. Turn the chair so its back is towards you (shorter students should turn the chair sideways) and take up fighting stance.

Use a mirror to check that you are kicking to the centre
Kick over the chair back

Use a chair to teach you to raise the knee high enough

Perform a front kick, lifting your foot over the back of the chair and retrieving it the same way afterwards.

Discussion

Co-ordination of the kicking movement is very important. For example, the supporting foot only stops swivelling as the foot strikes the target. Not only does this add a twisting (torsional) energy to the kick but it also increases range. Test this for yourself by using a partner.

Face the partner and, keeping your hips facing directly forward, perform a slow front kick. Your partner positions himself slightly out of range, so the kick won't quite reach. Repeat the kick but this time, swivel on your supporting foot and you will discover that the kick now reaches the target. This is because leading with the hip can add as much as 20 centimetres to the reach of a front kick.

You can also achieve extra range and impact by dragging the supporting leg forwards a short distance during the kick's delivery. Timing is critical and the drag forward must occur instants before the foot lands on the target. Forward

Slide forward on the supporting leg to gain power and range

Begin from fighting stance
Front and rear feet skip past each other

The kicking knee springs immediately on landing…
…and delivers front kick

movement resists recoil more effectively than any form of rigid stance.

Experienced martial artists can ignore the advice given earlier and spring the kicking foot up and forward with a heel-lifting action. Through practice, they quickly lift their foot into the correct path before the target is reached. This springing action gives a plyometric effect, especially when combined with a skipping movement.

The front and rear feet switch positions very quickly and the kick is launched even as the new rear foot settles. The calf muscle is first stretched quickly, then explosively contracted. The hips begin twisting, so the flexors are first stretched and then suddenly contracted. These two effects must be synchronised to achieve maximum force.

Use front kick carefully and only when a target presents itself. Some martial artists seem to throw kicks in the hope that they will find an opening. This strategy leads to injuries, as toes and shins bark against elbows and knees.

Kicks to the upper torso are more difficult to deflect because they zoom over the top of scooping blocks and lower parries. Add to the opponent's difficulty by kicking slightly to the side of his body's centre line.

Use front kicks carefully against an opponent known for his counter-attacks. If you try to kick him from close range, he will slide forward on his front leg and reverse-punch you as your knee is rising. How can you combat this? Feint at his face with your leading fist and simultaneously draw back your front foot. Your body is now not so close and his punch falls short.

Conversely, don't try front kick if you are slightly outside optimum distance, because you may overreach into a heavy and uncontrolled landing. An alert opponent will use this opportunity to sweep you.

Short Range Front Kick

Short range front kick develops virtually all of its power through leg movement alone. For this reason it is always advisable to kick with the back leg from a fighting stance. This provides both correct hip position and weight distribution for

Front kick is deflected by a number of blocks...

...but aiming the kick high and to the side makes it less easy to deal with

Use front kick carefully or…

…the opponent can slide forward and reverse-punch you

Over-reaching may result in a heavy, uncontrolled landing

rapid deployment. The guard remains stationary as the rear knee swings forward and up. The supporting foot only swivels slightly and the hips thrust forward. The kicking foot is quickly retrieved and returned to its original position.

Practise the kick in conjunction with a step forwards or a step backwards until you can do both with equal skill.

Front Kick to Head

This is performed as for a normal front kick except that the kicking knee is raised higher than before. The supporting knee remains slightly bent so it can adjust the centre of gravity, and the sole of the supporting foot remains flat on the floor.

Students who cannot comfortably manage front kick to the opponent's upper torso are not yet ready to try this kick, and should work on their hip flexors and hamstrings until enough flexibility is gained.

Lack of flexibility shows itself in an unwel-

Combat this by drawing back your leading foot before kicking

Now his reverse punch falls short

Take care not to raise the heel of the supporting foot

come modification of the technique. The knee does not fully extend, so range is reduced and impact force is squandered. The heel of the supporting leg may also rise, so stability and recoil-absorption suffer. A tendency to over-lean backwards must be avoided by bringing the knee closer to the chest before thrusting out the lower leg. The shoulders will be more likely to hunch up, so watch this. The higher the kick, the more there is a tendency to drop the guarding hands.

Snap kick to the jaw uses a similar action, except that the knee rises until it almost touches the chest. The lower leg thrusts upwards and out in an arc, striking beneath the opponent's jaw.

Front Leg Front Kick

Front kicks can be delivered with the leading leg. This is particularly useful if the opponent rushes forwards. A cat stance is the best to use because most body weight is already concentrated over the rear leg. The opponent's advance

increases both the force of impact and the resulting recoil.

Shift weight backwards from fighting stance and lift your leading knee as the opponent rushes in. Thrust out a front kick and set it back down to the outside of the opponent's foot, where he can't then sweep you.

Maintain an effective guard with both arms in the midline of the body.

Turning Front Kick

This is a variety of front kick in which the kicking hip lifts slightly during the last stages of delivery. The lower leg is half-way extended when hip movement displaces the foot outwards, so it strikes at an angle. It is in-between a front kick and roundhouse kick, though it is closer to the former.

Use it when the target is partially closed to a direct kick.

Twisting Kick

This is a second form of front kick in which the hip joint rotates slightly. Begin from fighting stance, bringing the rear knee up and forward – but do not swivel on the supporting foot. The kicking knee moves diagonally across the front of your body and as the lower leg is thrust out, the hip rotates outwards. This twists the kick into an outwards- and upwards-travelling path. The upper body leans into the kick, to cope with recoil.

Use twisting kick to attack targets closed to a direct front kick. The value of the technique lies in its novelty, for it is seldom seen. It generates less power than roundhouse kick and is most effectively used against the opponent's jaw.

Begin from fighting stance Bring the kicking knee diagonally up and forward, across the front of your body

The foot moves into an upward and outwards-travelling path

Use twisting kick to attack targets closed to a normal front kick

Raise your knee and…

…twist the foot around and into the target

One Step Front Kick

One step front kick uses a scissors step to accelerate forward movement and to close distance. The length of the step must be judged carefully because one that is too long drags out the scissors stance and slows the kick; too short a step may not close distance sufficiently.

Begin from fighting stance by sliding the rear foot forwards and turning it outwards. Lift the kicking foot and thrust it into the target. Retrieve the kick as usual and set it down carefully.

The following faults are commonly associated with one step front kick:

- the transition from scissors step to kick is jerky; this eventually smoothes out as skill improves,
- the shoulders have a greater tendency to hunch during the scissors step; use a mirror to detect and eliminate this fault,
- the guard has a tendency to flap about during the step,
- the knees have a habit of straightening during the step so you bob up and down; use the mirror to check this,
- the front foot of the scissors step sometimes

does not twist outwards so the hips are not aligned properly and range is reduced,
- control over the centre of gravity is lost and the kicking leg thumps down after retrieval; weight must always be kept over the supporting leg, using a slight backward lean to counter the mass of the kicking leg.

Slide the rear foot forward and twist it outwards

The step acts as an accelerator, making the kick more powerful

It is never a good idea to take an undisguised step towards the opponent. Use a feint to the face, so his attention is adequately diverted. Fast, straight punches make particularly effective feints. Nevertheless, the step forwards remains a weakness so the faster you make it, the greater the chance of success. A skip forwards is faster than a step and when you synchronise with the kick, the result is very powerful.

Skipping kicks come in between normal kicks and jumping kicks. Unlike the latter, the skipping kick strikes home whilst the supporting foot is in contact with the floor.

The lower the flight path, the more effective the skip. Skip forward with the rear foot as though intending to make a scissors step but begin the kick even as the foot is settling. Do not wait until all momentum is shed. With so much forward movement, extra care is needed to keep the centre of gravity under control.

Don't restrict skipping kicks to simple forward advances. They are even more effective when you skip diagonally to open your opponent's body, whereas previously it was closed to direct advance.

6
Front Stamping and Barring Kicks

General Features of Kicks

Front stamping and barring kicks all use the sole and/or heel of the foot to strike the opponent.

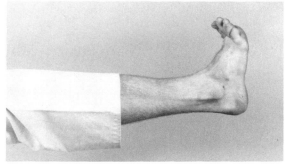

Stamping/barring kicks use the heel and sole of the foot

Delivery is similar to that of a front kick except that most power is generated in the thrusting out of the lower leg in a piston-like movement. The kicking knee is raised until it is generally above the target before the foot is driven out.

Part of Foot Used

These kicks all use the sole of the foot and/or the heel, with the ankle fully flexed. The ball of the foot faces upwards or slightly to one side or the other. At no time is the heel at the same level. That fact distinguishes these from the side kicks.

Front-stamping Kick to Midsection

Except for the different foot configuration, this technique is performed in a similar way to the

Begin from fighting stance

Raise the kicking knee higher than the target

Straighten the knee and thrust out the kicking foot

Step to one side, withdraw the trailing leg   Raise the kicking knee   Thrust out the foot

Side-step to evade the opponent's attack   Maintain an effective guard and raise the kicking knee

Keep control over your centre of gravity…

…otherwise you may fall into your opponent

Thrust the foot into the opponent's hip joint

short range front kick described in the previous chapter. The kicking knee is brought forwards and raised slightly above the target height. The foot then thrusts slightly downwards as the supporting foot twists.

Use this kick to drive the attacker backwards and into range of either an axe kick or roundhouse kick.

A second version uses a sideways evasion to avoid the opponent's attack. Step to one side and draw up the other foot. Raise the knee whilst maintaining an effective posture. Thrust out the kicking foot and strike the opponent's hip joint using power generated by the leg muscles. Keep the centre of gravity over the supporting leg, so there is no tendency to fall into the opponent.

Step to one side   Raise the kicking knee   Thrust the foot out heel-first

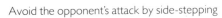

Avoid the opponent's attack by side-stepping   Raise the knee which is closest to the opponent

Raise your foot and simply 'plant' it in the opponent's midsection as he rushes forward

Don't lead with your chin

Kick the knee which is closest to you

Front-stamping Kick to Knee

Practise this in conjunction with a sideways evasion. Step to one side and draw in the other foot. Lift your knee and strike downwards onto the opponent's kneecap. This is a close-range kick, so use the foot nearest to the opponent.

Front Barring Kick to Midsection

This simple kick uses an economy of movement to stop the opponent's advance. As he rushes forward, simply lift your leg and plant the sole of your foot in his midsection. Thrust your hips slightly forward but keep the back of your head in a vertical line with the heel of the supporting foot.

The knee is already half extended when raised and the kick relies upon the opponent's forward momentum. Brace yourself against recoil and don't hunch your body forward.

7
Groin Kick

There are two versions of groin kick, one of which is midway between a front kick and a roundhouse kick. Otherwise this technique may be thought of as a form of snap kick, where the hips play little part and most power is generated by the muscles of the upper leg and lower stomach. The foot is fully extended, so the instep lies in one line with the shin, and the toes are turned down slightly.

Not much power is required because the groin is such a sensitive area, so groin kick can be delivered equally well from front or rear foot. One-step versions are common.

Begin from left fighting stance, carrying your hands in a relaxed yet effective guard. Bring your right knee quickly up and forwards, whilst swivelling on the supporting leg. If you intend to drop forward after the kick, then it may be a

good idea to change your guard. Otherwise, simply maintain the guard which you begin with. The kicking knee accelerates to a height which is just above the level of the opponent's groin.

Just as this height is reached, snap out your lower leg, in an upward swing to the opponent's groin. Maintain balance by leaning back slightly, otherwise you may fall into him. Keep your shoulders low and do not wave your arms about.

Adopt the correct range and angle before kicking, or you may injure your toes through over-extension on impact.

The second version of this technique is used when the opponent's groin is not open to a direct kick. The kicking hip lifts, so the foot passes diagonally around the opponent's guarding thigh.

8
Roundhouse Kick

General Features of Kick

Roundhouse kick takes either the ball of the foot or the instep in a circular path that runs almost parallel to the floor in the final instants before impact. The muscles of the upper leg and hips generate the power, the latter also determining the angle at which the foot travels. The kick is augmented by a torsional twist of the spinal column set up by rotating the shoulders in the direction of the kick and momentarily preventing the hips from following.

Some schools teach novices to raise their kicking foot to the side, and then to twist around on the supporting leg. However, roundhouse kick isn't actually delivered in that manner. The kicking foot moves upwards and outwards

Roundhouse kick uses either the ball of the foot or the instep in a circular movement

The kicking foot moves outwards as the supporting foot rotates

A good compromise swings the knee quickly across the body

Note that body lean is greater than that used in front kick

simultaneously, the relative degrees of each varying with the progress of the kick. Furthermore, it is not a good idea to alert the opponent to the technique you intend using, so you should disguise the kick until the last possible moment.

To be sure, some versions of roundhouse kick are completely unrecognisable until the lower leg is thrust out. Whilst these are excellent for miscueing the opponent, they unfortunately lack impact power because a part of the hip action is deliberately delayed.

A good compromise swings the knee quickly across the front of the body, so would-be attackers are fended off. The upper body leans back, so hip action is unimpeded and the weight of the kicking leg is balanced. Note that body lean in roundhouse kick is far greater than in front kick. This is because the foot follows a circular path and an extended upper body soaks up recoil more effectively.

The most powerful roundhouse kicks are delivered with the rear leg, though it is possible to perform a fairly effective front leg kick which makes contact with the temple, jaw, or throat.

A height limiting factor for roundhouse kick is the degree of abduction your hip joint will allow.

The degree of hip abduction which you can manage effectively limits the height of your roundhouse kick

This is the name given to the action of lifting your foot out to the side of your body. Less limiting is the degree of hamstring stretch available.

Parts of Foot Used

The instep is an ideal weapon for attacking the groin, thighs and the side of the jaw. The foot is extended until the instep is in line with the shin. The toes curl down out of harm's way. Impact occurs on that part of the instep nearest to the ankle. Contact closer to the toes may painfully overextend them.

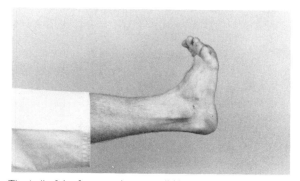

The ball of the foot produces a solid impact

It is particularly effective against the opponent's jaw

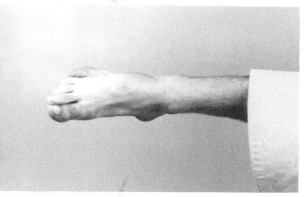

The instep is an ideal weapon for attacking the groin, thighs and…

…the side of the jaw

The technique must be aimed accurately because a badly bruised foot occurs all too frequently when the instep collides with the opponent's knee or elbow.

The ball of the foot is also used, and though it may be psychological, one feels that it has a slightly shorter range. Actually, ball of foot roundhouse produces a far more effective impact.

Begin from fighting stance

Turn your shoulders and bring the kicking knee forward and up

Foot configuration is slightly different to that used in front kick. The toes are pulled back as before, but the ankle is now flexed, so the instep is at 90° to the shin.

Roundhouse Kick to Midsection

Begin from fighting stance by rotating your shoulders in the direction of the kick and lifting the rear foot from the floor. The ankle is not directly below the knee, as it was with front kick; rather it lifts to the side. Change your guard over at this point, maintaining a viable defensive posture. Keep the elbows close to your sides. Twist on your supporting leg so the knee comes around and across the front of your body, where it can be used to fend off an opponent. It will be easier to pivot on the supporting leg if you slightly lift the heel.

Allow the hips freedom to move by leaning away from the rising kick. The kicking hip actually rolls up and over the top of the supporting hip and the lower leg thrusts out as the kicking knee swings around to point at the target. Strike the target with either ball of foot or instep, retrieve it and set it down.

Don't hinge your body forward as you kick. Swivel your supporting leg by at least a right angle. Bring your knee to the correct height and do not kick up in a diagonal manner. Don't swing your knee too far across your body or you may over-rotate and land in a vulnerable position.

Twist on your supporting foot

The kicking hip rolls up and over the supporting hip

The lower leg is thrust out

Faults to Watch Out For

The following are typical faults encountered in roundhouse kick:

Body weight is biased over the kicking leg, so a body shift is necessary to allow the kick to be used.	Kick from a stance with suitable weight bias. Use cat stance for front foot kicks and fighting stance for back leg kicks.
The guard is not changed during an advancing kick, so you land in an open posture.	Change guard hands over during kick. Novices will find it easier to change guard at the beginning, when the shoulders are turning.
The kick appears jerky.	Relax shoulders and aim for a smooth action. The body is relaxed rather than tense.

The arms fly out during the kick.	Keep the arms relaxed and hold the elbows to your sides with a minimum of muscle action.
The foot lifts to the side while the upper body is still upright.	Begin to twist the upper body before the foot rises. Bring the knee quickly across the front of the body.
The kick travels in a diagonally upward path.	The supporting foot has not swivelled sufficiently. The knee has not abducted to the correct height. The ankle of the kicking foot has dropped so it is below the height of the knee.

The kick travels diagonally upwards

The knee drops until it is pointing downwards

The kicking knee drops until it is pointing downwards.	The hips are insufficiently flexible. Stretch the thigh adductors with the exercises given. Use a chair to train hip abduction.
The kicking action is jerky because the lower leg is thrust out only after the hips have stopped swivelling.	Synchronise kicking action so the lower leg begins to thrust out before the hips have stopped swivelling.

The body does not lean away but is hinged forward at the waist. This reduces the ability to cope with recoil.	Continue the initial twisting action of the shoulders so the body leans back away from possible counters. Use a plastic pole to help position the body.
The martial artist appears to bob up and down during a series of kicks.	Keep the supporting leg bent during the kick.
The instep is not fully extended and the foot flops about.	Extend the toes fully to reduce risk of injury. Train by kneeling down for periods of time.
Impact is made with the extended toes.	Close range and strike with front of ankle.
The body falls forward as the kick is withdrawn and the kicking foot slaps down hard on the floor.	Control over the body's centre of gravity has been lost. Lean back to balance kicking leg.

Training Aids

Use a mirror to check that:

- your kicking knee comes quickly across the front of your body,
- your upper body is leaning away from a possible attack,
- your head is raised, so you can clearly see the opponent,

- your shoulders do not hunch,
- you retain an effective guard throughout,
- your knee rises to the correct height.

Use a punch-bag or impact pad to check that:

- your foot is correctly configured,
- you strike the bag with the correct part of your foot,
- you generate sufficient impact force,
- you can withstand recoil.

Use a mirror to check that your head is raised

Use target mitts:

- to improve accuracy,
- to improve reaction speed,
- to learn how to control impact (important for non-contact martial art competition).

A chair can be used to confirm that your foot is lifting sufficiently. A lightweight plastic pole is useful for ensuring that you lean back during the kick. Your partner holds the pole a few centimetres from your chest. Kick so your body twists and pulls away from it.

Discussion

It is impossible to perform a technically good roundhouse kick if you lack the flexibility to abduct your kicking knee sufficiently. Any attempt made without this flexibility will result in an unacceptably modified technique. People with inflexible hips often lean back overmuch and though this can produce the desired elevation, it makes the kick both unstable and slow to recover.

Use target mitts to develop accuracy

A lightweight pole is useful for providing feedback…

…in the matter of body lean

Roundhouse kick travels in a circular path, so it covers a greater distance than front kick and faces an increased likelihood of detection. On the other hand, it approaches from the side and unless the opponent turns his head to see it clearly, it can slip in unnoticed. Surprisingly, this tends to happen more often when the kick is travelling relatively slowly. Perhaps the absence of apparent muscular exertion combined with an indirect attack path lulls the opponent into disregarding it.

Roundhouse kick is particularly susceptible to what is called 'line'. This term describes the relative positions that you and the opponent occupy. Imagine that both of you face each other in left fighting stance. Then imagine you are looking down from vertically overhead at the positions of the leading feet. In the first case, your front foot is in line with his rear foot and vice versa. In the second case, your front foot is in line with his front foot.

The first case allows the opponent to slide his front leg forward and to reach you with reverse punch or front kick as you begin to raise your kicking knee. The second case places you slightly to his outside, so he must now twist or step in order to reach you. Try this out for yourself and see what I mean. However, don't take your body too far out of line or the opponent will notice it and re-position himself.

Take extra care also when using a rear leg roundhouse kick against opponents who fight southpaw. No matter how good your line, you are bound to turn square-on and present a good target. Either slide the front foot back before you kick, or step diagonally forward and out of line with your leading foot before kicking. Step-up roundhouse kick is a third alternative which we will consider a little later in the chapter.

Use roundhouse kick when your opponent is circling you. Aim against the direction he is moving, so he travels onto the kick and adds to its impact. Don't kick in the same direction he is circling or you may need to over-rotate on your supporting leg.

Skip-kicking develops speed and agility. Switch feet quickly and kick immediately the ball of the rear foot contacts the floor.

Sometimes roundhouse kick is not blocked because it approaches from the side

Although I described 'diagonal roundhouse kick' as an imperfect technique, in the hands of an expert it is actually very effective. This is because it travels a relatively short distance. However, accuracy is needed to avoid the opponent's elbows and shoulders.

As the opponent faces you in left fighting stance, you will see only a small target area below his left elbow. Above and below this, the left side of his body is shielded successively by his shoulder, arm, hip and thigh. Compare this with the right side, where a broad swathe of chest and ribs is open to attack. For this reason the left side is referred to as 'closed' and the right as 'open'. It obviously makes more sense to attack the open side.

Take extra care when using roundhouse kick against a southpaw

Draw your front foot back...

The opponent's left side provides few opportunities for a clean impact

The kick must clear the opponent's leading arm and shoulder in order to reach his head

Midsection Roundhouse Kick with Ball of Foot

This is very similar to the previous technique. Angle of delivery is important and every effort must be made to lift the kicking foot to the same height as the knee. For best technique, impact is made with the heel marginally higher than the ball of the foot.

Lift the foot to virtually the same height as the kicking knee

...and kick. His reverse punch now misses

Power the foot all the way in to the target

The opponent's right side presents more opportunities

The foot is powered all the way to the target and some teachers use an additional pushing movement of the foot on impact.

Roundhouse Kick to Head with Instep

This is the most commonly used head kick. Do not attempt it until you have the necessary hip flexibility. Novices generally fail to lift the kicking knee high enough with the result that the technique travels diagonally upwards and glances off an upper arm or shoulder. A correct delivery takes the foot over the opponent's shoulder.

The kick is performed in the same way as the midsection equivalent except that the kicking knee is raised much higher and more body lean is used. People lacking hip mobility always begin to extend the lower leg early in the kick so that by the time it reaches the correct height, the entire leg is virtually straight and closing on the target through ballistic hip rotation.

The straighter leg generates more momentum and this has the effect of slightly increasing flexibility in a trained person. This modification

Roundhouse kick to the head using the instep is probably the most commonly used head kick

Begin from fighting stance

Twist your shoulders and hips, and raise the kicking knee

Swivel on your supporting leg

is regarded by some martial artists as generally unacceptable, though as any follower of Thai boxing knows, it is also highly effective. However, the ballistically augmented straight-leg roundhouse kick is very difficult to retrieve and a suitable follow-up technique must always be on hand.

Powerful head kicks cause the supporting heel to rise.

Roundhouse Kick to Head Using Ball of Foot

This kick is similar to the previous technique except that still more hip flexibility is needed to take the foot slightly higher than the target. Pay special attention to the arms, which are prone to wave about.

In some schools, the body remains upright during the kick. This requires very flexible hips and leaves the torso open to counter. On the credit side, it is a fast kick and allows you to counter or to follow through your attack without having to first restore the body's equilibrium.

Divert attention with an effective and powerful reverse punch to the opponent's midsection. As the punch extends, weight comes off the rear leg, so it can be lifted up. Time the roundhouse kick to make contact just as the spent reverse punch is pulled back.

The low punch focuses attention downwards and creates a window of opportunity for the high roundhouse kick. Having said that, the window remains open for only a short time, so the kick must follow quickly behind the punch.

Competition Roundhouse Kick

Competition roundhouse kick needs maximum speed but not maximum power. This means that it can be modified. Begin from fighting stance, springing the foot up and forwards, as though you were performing front kick. The toes, however, point to the floor. The supporting foot does not begin to twist until much later than usual.

It follows that though the opponent realises you intend to kick, he will not be clear at this point which kick you will use.

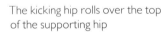
The kicking hip rolls over the top of the supporting hip

Thrust out the lower leg

The spent kick is quickly withdrawn

Divert the opponent's attention with a reverse punch to midsection

Begin the roundhouse kick as the reverse punch is withdrawn

Begin as for front kick

Partially thrust out the lower leg

The supporting leg begins to swivel

The supporting leg begins to swivel powerfully as the lower leg is snapped out. This causes a last-minute shift in the angle of delivery so the foot switches to a rising diagonal arc into the target. Lean back from a possible counter-attack, turn your toes down and impact with controlled force. Train by attacking a target mitt held at the maximum height which you can reach.

As you become more skilled, the hip rotation which changes the attack angle can be further delayed. Eventually, the technique looks for all the world like a front kick, but as the opponent moves to scoop it, the foot suddenly flicks up and smacks him in the ear. This is a truly effective technique and is well worth the effort needed to learn it.

The corollary of this is rare, though it does sometimes occur in competition. The round-house kick looks set up when all of a sudden the kicking foot drops below the knee and front kick is delivered. Try it against a punch-bag.

The kick strikes only instants after the punch is withdrawn, so the opponent has little time to deal with the new attack

| The foot swings outwards and up | The lower leg is thrust out… | …and the foot makes contact |

The opponent sees what he thinks is a front kick and moves to block it

However, the kick lifts over the intended block…

Begin from fighting stance

Raise the front knee and tilt the hips

Begin to thrust out the lower leg

Strike with either the ball of the foot or the instep

...and strikes the opponent's head

Front foot roundhouse kick is effective from close range

Front Foot Roundhouse Kick

This is not a particularly powerful technique, though it works well in non-contact competition. It is best delivered from either a cat stance or a back stance. Raise the kicking knee to the correct height and point it at the target. Your foot is also raised so it is diagonally behind and below the knee. The supporting leg twists around as the lower leg is thrust out and the upper body leans away from counter-attack. Impact is made with either the ball of the foot or the instep.

Long Range Roundhouse Kick

Increase the range of your rear foot roundhouse kick by dragging forward on the bent supporting leg as the kicking knee swings up to effective height. The moving knee provides energy for the drag forward. The extending lower leg releases additional ballistic energy.

Extend range still further with a scissors step past the front leg. Twist the stepping foot outwards as it sets down to set up the hips correctly for a fast kick. Adjust the step length to suit the circumstances and use a feint to disguise

Raise your knee high enough so the foot can clear the opponent's shoulder...

Extent range with a scissors step

Synchronize completion of the step with a fast knee-raise

Lean back for maximum range

Begin from fighting stance

Slide the rear foot forward

Raise the kicking knee

the movement. Remember to keep your legs bent throughout, so your body doesn't bob up and down. Hold the guard in a relaxed but effective manner.

Step-up roundhouse kick provides a fast but less powerful alternative for closing distance. Begin from fighting stance and jab forwards with your leading fist into the opponent's face. Make the punch effective, so the opponent is forced to pull his face back and perhaps block. Throw weight over your leading leg and slide the back leg forward at the same time. Provided that you punch and step up quickly, your opponent may not see it.

As you withdraw your fist, throw a fast front leg roundhouse kick at the opponent's jaw. Don't leave too much of a gap between pulling back the fist and delivering the kick. Keep your supporting knee bent.

Double Kicks on Same Leg

This is an excellent training method for acquiring skill. It teaches good form, co-ordination and correct balance, though the kicks do not develop maximum power. Use a target mitt.

Begin from fighting stance and bring your rear foot forward and into a roundhouse kick to midsection. Use either ball of foot or instep. Pull the foot back after impact and rather than setting it down, lean back further and raise your kicking knee higher, so it points to head height. Twist your supporting foot outward a little more as the hips rotate further. Thrust out your lower leg for a second kick. Retrieve and set it down carefully.

Note that it is easier to kick first to midsection and then to the head, than it is to do the reverse. This is because roundhouse kick to the head requires considerable hip action, leaving none for the midsection kick.

Adopt fighting stance and accelerate your rear knee up and forward, so it is pointing to midsection. Thrust out your lower leg and perform front kick. Keep your elbows to your sides and control the centre of gravity, so you both extend and withdraw the kick without losing balance. Thrust the foot out a second time but turn/lean your upper body away and twist

Thrust out the lower leg, this time striking with the instep

Withdraw the kick and set it down

Disguise the step-up with a snap punch to the face

Use the window created to strike home with roundhouse kick

Roundhouse kick to midsection leaves enough hip twist in reserve…

…to perform a second kick on the same leg – this time to the head

Thrust out your lower leg in a front kick

Withdraw the kick and tilt your hips

Thrust out your lower leg once more, this time in a roundhouse kick

further on the supporting leg. Raise the kicking hip and so perform a roundhouse kick. Depending upon your flexibility, aim the second kick either to midsection or to the head.

The second kick must be performed smoothly and be withdrawn without loss of balance.

The martial artist who has truly mastered this technique can kick slowly without losing his balance. Less skilled students can only perform the techniques quickly, relying on sheer speed to mask errors in performance and balance.

A skilled martial artist can kick slowly without losing balance

9
The Side Kick

General Features of Kick

Side kick is a powerful, thrusting kick that drives the heel into the target from a sideways-on body position. It is very powerful and works equally well from short, medium and long range. Fastest delivery is made from the front leg, and unlike most other kicks, there is little loss of power.

Though there are several ways of performing the kick, I believe that one method yields significantly higher impact force, though I cannot as yet prove this objectively.

As a general principle, side kick is powered by a combination of knee and hip extension, coupled with rotation of the hips and an added thrust through the centre of gravity. This is difficult to synchronise, so many novices first

Side kick is a powerful technique in which the heel is driven into the target from a sideways-on body position

Side kick works well from short distance . . .

turn their hips, then thrust the foot out. This is slow, hesitant, and robs the technique of power.

Side kick does require a high order of hip flexibility, especially in the directions of abduction and rotation. High side kicks require great flexibility and skill. The angle of the hips is critical and unless set up right, the ability to absorb recoil is seriously reduced.

Part of Foot Used

Side kick strikes with the heel of the foot. Less powerful strikes can be made with the outer edge of the foot (that part which runs from the base of the little toe to the heel). Some martial art schools use the sole of the foot, but this is less efficient in transmitting energy. Test this for yourself by pressing the palm of your hand against your chest. Repeat this, but now use the middle joint of the fully flexed thumb. The second version is more painful because the same

High side kick requires good flexibility

...middle distance...

...and long distance...

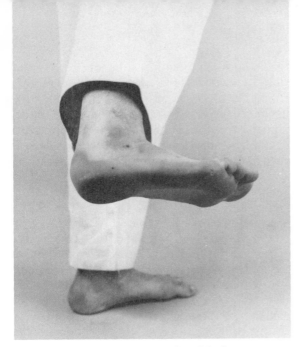

amount of force is channelled through a smaller area of contact.

To get the correct configuration, hold your foot so the sole is flat to the floor. Extend your leg fully and lift the big toe whilst turning the others down. The heel leads the edge of the foot and the ball of foot faces slightly downwards. Some people find difficulty in lifting one toe and turning down the others. However, after a little practice, this soon becomes possible.

Side Kick to Midsection

Until this point, kicks off the front foot have been generally less powerful. As I mentioned in the introduction to this chapter, this is not the case with side kick. Begin from a straddle stance with feet a shoulder-width apart or so. Hold your fists in a relaxed guard position.

Side kick uses the heel and outer edge of the foot

Begin from a high straddle stance

Step up with the rear foot and raise the kicking knee at the same time

Thrust the heel into the target

Keep your eyes on the opponent

Lean back to counter the weight of your kicking leg

Thrust the kick into the target in a straight line

The classic guard extends one arm along the top of the kicking leg while the other folds across the chest

Step up with the rear leg; at the same time lift the leading foot straight off the floor to the correct height. Synchronise the movement so that the kicking knee raises the instant the step-up completes. The kicking foot points towards the opponent, from which position it is thrust diagonally upwards into the target.

Lean back to counterbalance the weight of your extending leg and swivel on the supporting foot until your back has virtually turned towards the opponent. The supporting leg must remain bent while the foot rotates more than 90°. Keep your eyes on the opponent and maintain an effective guard throughout. If you kick with the left leg, then typically your left arm extends above it. The right elbow flexes so the fist is carried across your chest. However, as long as an effective guard is maintained, its precise form is unimportant. Pull your whole leg back to your chest before setting it down.

The object is to drive the foot diagonally upwards and out; not to swing it in an upwards arc. The latter movement has no penetration.

The second way to practise side kick is by using the rear leg from a fighting stance. This is

Use a fighting stance to deliver a side kick from the rear leg

more difficult because the body rotates from three-quarters-on one way to fully sideways-on the other. Keep your arms close to your sides as you bring your back leg forwards and up, the foot hanging vertically below the knee. Draw the knee across the front of your body and swivel on the supporting foot, raising the kicking foot at the same time. Even as this is happening, thrust out the lower leg and lean back to maintain balance.

Typically, one arm extends above the kicking leg and the other folds across your chest. Contact is made in the last few degrees of supporting foot rotation, when the knee is almost fully extended. Withdraw the spent kick by folding the knee back against the chest and then setting it down.

I mentioned earlier that there is yet another way to perform side kick, whether with front leg or rear leg. This involves lifting the kicking knee as before but this time, the foot is raised so it actually points at the target. The kicking action now becomes an almost straight-line thrust of unexpected power, aided by a projection of the hips in the direction of the kick. Compare this action with that previously described. If the foot begins from a low position, then it must thrust diagonally upwards to reach the target. This may reduce penetration and weaken the kick.

Try this version either from straddle stance or from fighting stance. Raise the kicking knee whilst pulling the big toe up and turning the other toes downwards. Draw the knee diagonally across the front of your body and pivot on the supporting leg at the same time. Thrust your hips into the kick as you drive the heel out.

The Southern Shaolin schools use a short range front foot side kick to vulnerable targets exposed following an evasion movement. After avoiding and deflecting the attack, lift the foot closest to the opponent until the kicking foot is nearly at the height of the target. Then drive out the edge of the foot and heel, using a thrusting action of the kicking leg. Note that the hips are not rotated as far as in the previous forms, though some body lean remains essential to balance the kick. Without this, you may well fall forward into the opponent and suffer the consequences. A viable guard is very important.

Keep your arms close to your sides and draw the kicking knee up and across your body

Thrust out the kicking foot

Lift your foot and point it at the target

Thrust your foot in a straight line using leg extension

Southern Shaolin schools use a sideways evasion…

…to avoid the opponent's attack

The foot closest to the target is lifted…

…and thrust into the target

Use this technique from close range

Evade the attack by the minimum safe distance

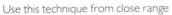

Without lean-back, you may lose control over your centre of gravity…

…and fall forward into the opponent

The kick travels the shortest possible distance

The body leans back and an effective guard is maintained

The Shotokan school of karate uses an interesting version of side kick in which the edge of the foot glances across the opponent's ribs, rather than thrusting into them. This kick is performed as per normal except that impact is with the edge of the foot, and not with the heel.

Side kick can also be used with a slicing action that cuts the edge of the foot across the target

Faults to Watch Out For

The following general faults occur in side kick practice:

Body weight is biased over the kicking leg, so a shift of balance is needed to allow the leg to be used. This can warn the opponent.	Kick from a stance with a neutral weight bias, or step-up and kick, so weight lifts off the kicking foot.
The guard does not change during an advancing kick, so you land in an open posture.	Change guard naturally as the body leans back. Extend the leading hand above the kicking leg and tuck the other across your chest.
The kick appears jerky.	Try for a smooth transition of power, with no hesitations or stiff upper body. Acceleration should increase through the technique.
The kicking knee does not lift high enough, so the lower leg must swing upwards to attain height.	A diagonal lift of the foot is in order, but this assumes that the knee is high enough. Use the exercises given and test by raising the foot over a chair back.

The kicking knee is not lifted high enough…   …so the lower leg swings up instead of thrusting out

The body does not lean back, so hip action is inhibited.	Lean back so that, seen from the front, you look like the letter 'Y', with the supporting leg as the upright and the kicking leg and upper body as the 2 arms.
The supporting leg straightens, so ability to absorb recoil is lost and you bob up and down.	Keep the supporting leg bent throughout.
The supporting foot does not twist past 90°, so the hips cannot extend the kick fully and the kicking foot strikes with the edge of the foot.	The supporting foot must rotate by at least 90°, so the hips are freed to drive the foot heel-first into the target.
The foot is not configured properly so it makes contact with the sole.	The heel makes first contact and the ball of the foot is carried slightly lower. Practise pulling up the big toe and turning down the others. Stiffen your ankle on impact.
The foot is not pulled back to the body afterwards, so the opponent can grasp hold of it.	Pull the spent kick back strongly.

The supporting leg does not twist sufficiently so the foot strikes with the outer edge, rather than the heel

The foot is not configured properly, so it makes contact with the sole

Control over the centre of gravity is lost and you fall forwards after retrieving the kick.

Use the lean-back to counter ballistic effects generated by the pull-back.

Training Aids

Use a mirror to check that:

- you are keeping your head up, especially during the lean-back,
- your shoulders aren't hunching up,
- your supporting leg remains bent and the foot rotates fully,
- your hips thrust into the kick,
- you recover posture quickly and smoothly.

Use a punch-bag to check that:

- your foot is correctly configured,
- you are striking directly into the target, and not slicing up past it,
- you are generating impact force,
- you can cope with recoil effects.

Use a chair back to confirm that you are lifting your knee high enough and a plastic pole to ensure proper lean-back and guard.

Discussion

Front leg side kick is both fast and powerful. Also, because it is relatively indifferent to range, it works well against an opponent who steps straight back. The combination of thrusting/ twisting hip action extends the kick and if a drag forwards is also used, the kick will seem to go on reaching out for ever. At the other end of the spectrum, the kick works well when your leading foot creeps inside your partner's. Providing weight distribution is right, the front foot lift-off can be masked by a feint to the face, such as back

Front foot side kick is both fast...

...and powerful

fist. The body leans well back out of harm's way. Aim high into the opponent's torso, and slightly off-centre, so the kick becomes difficult to block.

Another advantage of side kick is the strength of the foot weapon used. The heel is well padded and even if it misses the target and strikes bone, you are unlikely to suffer injury.

Side Kick to Knee

This is a very dangerous technique which suffers from accuracy problems. Great care must be taken when practising it with a partner.

It may be delivered from the front leg (with or without a step-up) or from the rear leg. Use either fighting stance or straddle stance. Lift the kicking knee and point your heel at the opponent's kneecap. Drive your foot straight down whilst twisting the hips and leaning away. Allow your supporting foot to rotate fully. Withdraw the kicking foot afterwards, setting it down carefully.

Wing Chun Kuen makes use of a sideways evasion which causes the opponent's attack to miss, yet leaves you close enough to respond immediately. The foot closest to the opponent is lifted so the heel points directly at his knee. It is then thrust down and into the target. An effective guard is essential. Attack whichever knee is closest and follow through with an effective concluding technique.

Body lean is essential insofar as your guard may not be as effective as you imagine it to be.

Side Kick to Head

This is definitely not a technique to attempt until your hips are sufficiently flexible. Kicking with a knee that is too low results in an upwards swinging kick rather than a thrust, and the ballistic effect this generates levers up the heel of the supporting foot, making it difficult to absorb recoil. There is also a tendency to drop the head. This must be avoided.

Wing Chun Kuen uses a sideways evasion…   …to avoid the opponent's attack   The knee closest to the opponent is raised…

Attack whichever knee…   …happens to be…

...and thrust down at the target

Body lean is essential...

...closest

...because your guard may not be quite enough on its own to deal with a punch

The kick is performed as for a midsection technique, with the obvious exception that the knee lifts higher and the body leans further. Few people can rotate their hips sufficiently in that position to point their heels actually at the target, so a degree of diagonal movement is inevitable. However, the higher the foot is raised, the greater the thrust achieved.

The kick is also characterised by extreme rotation of the supporting leg. In some cases it can turn up to 180° from straight ahead, so the kick is almost travelling out backwards.

The rear foot passes behind the front foot

The kick is characterised by extreme rotation of the supporting leg

One Step Side Kick

One step side kick uses a scissors step to accelerate body weight forwards. As in previous cases, the length of the step must be judged if maximum benefit is to be gained. This time the rear foot passes behind the front and the hips rotate so the back twists towards the target. This movement sets up the hips more effectively than stepping across the front of the supporting leg.

Synchronise actual delivery of the kick with

The kicking knee is raised in one smooth movement…

…and the kicking foot is thrust out

maximum momentum. Don't step, then hesitate, before thrusting the kick out. As you become more skilled, the step forwards becomes a skimming slide that sets the hips up on landing. Lean back as you step so the kick can be thrust out immediately the ball of the new leading foot touches down. Step back quickly and side kick. This is useful for staving off an advance and for building agility. With a little practice, you will be able to thrust out the kick as weight is settling after the spring back.

Double Side Kick on Same Leg

This develops skill and balance. Kick first to midsection, then withdraw the kick and thrust it out again to the head. The hips turn so far with the lower kick, and fully when kicking to the head. Kicking in the reverse order is more difficult for the reasons previously given.

Try also a three-kick combination on the same leg, commencing with front kick, passing to a roundhouse kick and finishing with side kick.

Begin from fighting stance

Raise the kicking knee

Thrust the kick out to midsection

Begin with front kick

Pull the spent kick back

Twist on the supporting leg

Withdraw the kick but don't set it down yet

Once more thrust out a side kick, this time to the head

Perform a roundhouse kick

Pull the spent kick back
and across your body

Thrust out a side kick

10
Back Kick

General Features of Kick

Back kick is very similar to side kick in that the heel is thrust directly into the target. They differ, however, in the extent to which the body is turned away from the opponent. Some schools teach back kick facing completely away from the opponent, whilst others teach students to crane the neck and look over the shoulder.

Back kick is technically difficult and requires a sense of keen spatial awareness – knowing where the opponent is in relation to your moving body.

Back kick and side kick are similar, differing only in the degree of hip twist used

The technique consists of two components, a turning motion of the body followed by a straight thrusting kick. Back kick is most effective when as little warning as possible is given to the opponent.

It isn't a good idea to turn one's back on the opponent since few body weapons can then be used. Nevertheless back kick is both powerful and effective over a range of distance. Ideally it is combined with a technique during which the hips are fully turned. For example, it follows both side kick and roundhouse kick as a natural extension of their movement.

Part of Foot Used

Back kick uses the same foot configuration as side thrust kick. The ball of the foot is pulled back and the heel projects furthest. However, the foot points vertically downwards, rather than being angled downwards as in the side kick. The big toe is lifted and the others are extended.

Back kick uses the heel. The ball of the foot faces downwards

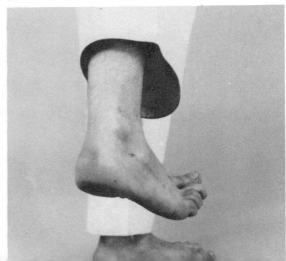

Back Kick to Midsection

Practise back kick from a fighting stance by sliding your leading foot so it crosses an imaginary line drawn straight ahead from your rear foot. Keep your body facing forwards until the correct distance is reached, then allow your hips

Begin from fighting stance

Slide the front foot across

First turn your shoulders and then your hips, so your back turns towards the opponent

Lean your body forwards and raise the leading leg from the floor

Thrust the heel out in a straight line

Draw back the spent kick and straighten up

Set down the kicking leg diagonally across from the other

Turn your hips and then your shoulders until you face the front once more

Step across, twist your hips and kick in one seamless movement

the spin-around to return you to forward-facing once more.

For those who prefer to see where they are kicking, step across from fighting stance as before, but this time turn your head and look over your shoulder. Thrust the kicking leg out and keep your eye on the target. This method alters the hip position, so the kicking foot does not turn down to the floor, though this is not then a fault.

No matter how quickly it is performed, the step across remains an unmistakeable clue, so you may wish to try a version of back kick that works without it. Begin from a narrow fighting stance. Twist your body around, looking over your shoulder as you lift the kicking foot. Thrust the foot directly backwards into the target and withdraw it sharply afterwards.

Do not attempt this version if your stance is too wide, otherwise your kick will be off centre. A narrow stance is not particularly stable, so don't spend too long in it before kicking.

and shoulders to rotate, so your back turns towards the opponent.

Lean your body forwards and raise the leading leg from the floor. Keep your arms to your sides and thrust the heel out in a straight line to the target. The knee of your kicking leg turns down to point at the floor. Draw back the spent kick while straightening up. Set the kicking foot down and complete the turn facing the opponent once more.

Once you can perform the moves without hesitation, try stepping across and turning your hips in one seamless movement. When this is achieved, tack the kick to the end. Finally tie in

Begin from a narrow stance   Spin around quickly

Begin from fighting stance

Step across and turn your head to look over your shoulder

Thrust the kick out and keep your eyes on the target

Lift the kicking leg

Thrust out the foot

Withdraw the spent kick

Faults to Watch Out For

The following are common faults associated with back kick:

Too wide an opening stance, so the step across becomes too obvious.	Begin from a normal or even slightly narrower stance.
Step across is laborious and slow.	Take weight off the front leg. Back stance is useful for this.
Step across by too much, so kick goes off centre.	Step across an equal distance from an imaginary line drawn forward from the rear foot.
Step across by too little, so kick goes off centre in the opposite direction.	See above.
The turn-around appears jerky.	Practise until your skill level allows you to smooth out any hesitation.
You can't see where you're kicking.	Turn your head sharply to look over your shoulder at the opponent.

Stepping across by the wrong amount causes the kick to go off-centre

The knee does not point to the floor so the foot is wrongly presented

The elbows flap about during the kick.	Hold them next to your sides in a relaxed but firm manner.
The body does not lean forwards as the kick thrusts out. This robs the kick of valuable height.	Lean well forwards to counter the weight of your extending leg. Keep your head up.
The kicking knee is not turned down to the floor, so the foot is not set up correctly.	Practise rotating the hip fully, so the upper leg twists as far as possible.
The kick makes contact through the sole of the foot.	Review the way the foot is configured and project the heel backwards.
The spent kick is set down with insufficient side step with the result that the forward-facing stance is too narrow.	Set down the kicking leg with adequate side step.

The spent kicking foot is set down with insufficient side-step...

...so the new forward-facing stance is too narrow

The spent kick is set down with excessive side step so the forward-facing stance is too wide.

Set your foot down with the correct degree of side step. This comes through practice.

This time the spent foot is set down with excessive side-step...

...so the resulting stance is too wide

Training Aids

Use a mirror to check that:

- you are stepping across the correct distance,
- your hips are rotating fully,
- your body is leaning forwards by the correct degree,
- your elbows are kept to your sides,
- the kick is on target.

Use a punch-bag to check that:

- your foot is correctly configured,
- your kick is on target,
- you are generating impact,
- you can absorb recoil.

Discussion

Think of back kick as generally being performed in conjunction with a feint of some kind to disguise the hip movement. For example, a roundhouse kick sets the hips up correctly to follow through with back kick. Do not withdraw the spent roundhouse kick as completely as you might otherwise do. Land well forward instead, and slightly narrower than usual. Make no move fully to recover your hips because the landing angle reduces lead-in to the back kick.

Roundhouse kick sets up the hips

Do not withdraw the spent kick as completely as usual; rather drop the foot forward, with the hips still partly twisted

Use this to give an early start to the back kick. Raise the kicking foot...

...and thrust backwards with it

Withdraw the kick in the usual way

Use the turning motion of the hips to power a final reverse punch

Side kick also sets up the hips ready for a back kick

Drop the foot down on the diagonal...

It is possible to perform back kick from punching range. Use a feint to distract the opponent...

Use the natural set of the turning hips to deliver a back fist, or a reverse punch. The side kick/back kick combination works well for the same reasons.

It is possible to perform an effective back kick from punching distance but having said that, I wouldn't recommend using it in one-point or three-point competition.

...thrust out a back kick...

...and complete the sequence with a reverse punch

...spin round...

...raise your foot and thrust it back into the opponent's midsection

Begin from fighting stance   Step diagonally back with the   Thrust the foot straight out
                                leading foot

Spring-back Back Kick

Like side kick, back kick can be used to stop-kick an opponent. Begin from fighting stance by stepping diagonally back with the leading foot.

Twist your head and pick up the leg you just stepped with, thrusting it straight back at the advancing opponent. Withdraw it promptly.

11
Reverse Roundhouse Kick

General Features of Kick

Reverse roundhouse kick is a spectacular technique normally targeted against the head. The foot hooks back into the target using a hip rotation that travels in the reverse direction to roundhouse kick; hence the name.

Method of delivery varies, with maximum power generated by a rear leg kick working through a full 180° of body rotation. This is often combined with a high roundhouse kick, so the hips are already partially rotated and the reverse roundhouse is then merely a logical extension of the turning motion. When practising the 180° kick with a partner, bear in mind that it is difficult to control.

The competition version sacrifices power for speed and short travel, using the front foot and a step-up motion coupled to only a few degrees of body rotation. This initially looks like a side kick, miscueing the opponent into expecting a straight thrust.

An intermediate version uses the rear leg but without excessive body torsion.

Part of Foot Used

Competition reverse roundhouse kick strikes with the sole of the extended foot as a concession to the opponent's well-being. The toes are

The foot hooks back into the target using a hip rotation that travels in the reverse way to roundhouse kick

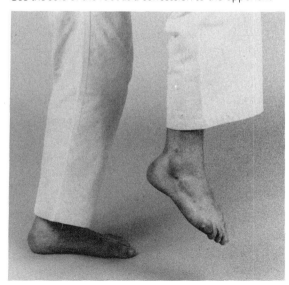

Use the sole of the foot as a concession to the opponent

Begin from fighting stance

Step up with the rear foot

Raise the kicking knee as though performing a side kick

Swing the kick out in an arc

Flex the knee as the kick passes the midline of your own body

Drop the kicking foot

turned downwards and the foot is arched. The full-power kick strikes with the heel – and I say again – take great care when using it against an opponent. Your ankle joint is flexed and the toes are relaxed.

Step-up Reverse Roundhouse Kick

This is the most used version of reverse round-house kick. Begin from fighting stance, sliding up with the rear foot and raising your kicking knee as though performing a side thrust kick. Swing the foot out in a shallow arc to the side of the opponent's head. Swivel on the supporting leg so the foot turns in the opposite direction to the kick. This action unrolls the kick and opens the hips.

The body leans back to counter the weight of the kicking leg and an effective guard is carried. The kicking knee flexes slightly and this is enough to bring the sole of the foot back and into the target. The spent kick is then retrieved as though it were a side thrust kick.

The kick travels to the target by hip action. The knee plays only a small part and the terminal hook-back must not be overemphasised.

Faults to Watch Out For

Weight is biased over the step-up leg, so an obvious body shift is first needed.	Put weight on the front leg, then it will be possible to step up quickly with the back leg.
The guard is changed during an advancing kick, leaving the body open upon landing.	As with all one-step kicks, hold the guard firmly yet relaxed during the step.

Hold the guard firmly, yet relaxed

The kick appears jerky.	Keep shoulders relaxed and train until the step-up/lift-off/kick sequence becomes seamless.
The elbows flap during the kick.	Hold guard firmly yet relaxed.
The knee does not lift high enough, so the kick is too low.	Stretch the thigh adductors with the exercises given. Lean back.
The supporting leg does not rotate fully, so the hips cannot be brought fully into play and impact is made with the ball of the foot pointing upwards.	The supporting leg must rotate so that the foot can be brought back into the opponent's head in the correct configuration.
The kicking knee flexes, so range is curtailed.	Hip action alone brings the foot into the target. The knee is extended.

The kicking knee must not flex excessively or range is lost

The body does not lean back far enough, so range is reduced.	Lean back fully to balance the leg but keep head raised and looking at opponent.
Control of centre of gravity is lost and kicking foot slaps down.	Gather knee to body after kick and then set it down.

Training Aids

Use a mirror to check that:

- you are raising the kicking knee high enough,
- you are leaning back sufficiently,
- your head is raised,
- your guard is effective,
- your supporting leg pivots fully,
- your kick extends.

Use a punch-bag to check that:

- your foot is configured correctly,
- your kick is striking into the bag,
- you are generating impact force,
- you can absorb recoil.

Use a target mitt to:

- improve accuracy, especially against a moving target,
- develop control so technique can be used in competition.

Reverse Roundhouse Kick from Rear Leg

There are two versions, both beginning from fighting stance. The first uses an outwards twist of the leading foot as the rear knee is brought forwards and up. At this stage, the technique could easily be mistaken for a side thrust kick. However, when the knee is raised high enough, the hips open out and the leg extends in the same way as that described above.

The second begins with the front foot sliding quickly across the front of the rear leg – exactly as though you were performing a back kick. However, instead of slowing body rotation to a stop and then thrusting out a straight kick, accelerate on through the turn. The almost straight kicking leg rises in a diagonal, up-wardstravelling circle and the heel (or sole of foot) strikes the target.

Pull your leg quickly back to the chest after contact is made and return to an effective fighting stance as soon as possible.

Discussion

The rear leg kick travels a great distance, during which time you are open to counter-attack. If you decide to use the kick alone, then make sure you begin from the correct distance and line. Otherwise the skilled opponent will move into the kick from your blind side, lifting you and reaping the supporting leg. The step-up version is far safer in this respect.

Face your partner in fighting stance and slide forwards on your front leg as you deliver a reverse punch to midsection. Bring your guard hand high across your chest and as the punch withdraws, use this hand to go over the top and strike with back fist to the opponent's face. This both disguises the step-up and throws weight forward, so the rear leg is free to slide. Lift the kicking knee quickly and deliver reverse round-house kick to the side of the opponent's face.

Begin from fighting stance

Slide the front foot across and swivel the body

The kicking leg is almost straight

Bring your body upright once more

Quickly adopt a new fighting stance

The hips then open out, and by this means they power the kick

Flex the knee before withdrawing it

Follow reverse punch with a back fist

Raise your kicking leg and deliver reverse roundhouse

12
Axe Kick

General Features of Kick

Axe kick is a spectacular and powerful technique, using muscle power, the mass of the extended leg and the force of gravity to drop the heel onto the opponent's head or collar bone.

There are various types of axe kick but all require good flexibility in the hamstrings.

It is virtually impossible to perform this technique correctly and still control it, so take great care when training with a partner.

Axe kick is a powerful technique used to attack the collarbones or the head

Begin from fighting stance

Swing the back foot forwards and up

The back arches and the hips thrust forward

Part of Foot Used

Classical axe kick is delivered with the heel of the foot. The ankle is strongly flexed, so the ball of the foot is pulled back and points upwards. The toes are flexed.

Sole of foot is used for your partner's safety. Fully extend your ankle and turn your toes downwards.

Vertical Axe Kick to Head

This is the most common version of the kick. Begin from fighting stance and swing the back leg forwards and up, as high as it will go. If your hamstrings are flexible, the kicking knee will actually bang against your shoulder. The knee joint must fully extend and the foot is pulled into the desired configuration. The back arches and your hips thrust forward. Bring the kicking foot slashing down but avoid slamming your heel into the floor.

Faults to Watch Out For

These are the major faults associated with axe kick:

The hamstrings are not flexible enough and the kick triggers a reflex muscle spasm.	Do not attempt this kick until you are sufficiently supple. The ballistic action can cause injury.
The foot catches the opponent as it is swung up.	The foot actually swings slightly wide of the body becoming truly vertical only at the shoulder.
The knee does not extend fully.	You have insufficient flexibility. Select from the exercises given earlier.
The foot flops about on the end of the kicking leg.	Pull the foot into the correct configuration.
The shoulders hunch up as the leg is swung high.	Relax your shoulders – they play no part in the kicking process.
The arms swing away from the sides.	Hold the elbows close to sides in a relaxed yet firm way.

Use a mirror to ensure that the kicking leg swings to a vertical position

Training Aids

Use a mirror to check that:

- the kicking leg swings to a vertical position,
- the kicking knee is fully extended,
- the foot is correctly configured,
- the shoulders are not hunched up,
- the arms are kept to the sides.

Use an impact pad to check that:

- you are striking with the correct part of your foot,
- you are generating impact force.

Do not rest the pad on top of your shoulder because an inaccurate kick may land on your head. Hold the pad by its straps and be prepared to have it jarred from your hands.

Discussion

Axe kick is rather more than a simple swing up/drop down action. You must also reach towards the opponent, and this is done by arching your

Face the opponent in fighting stance

Snap punch with your leading fist

Reverse punch immediately the snap punch is withdrawn

Swing your kicking leg up and drop it on the target

Axe kick is more than a simple swing up/swing down action

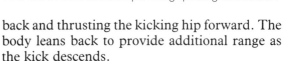

Diagonal axe kick chops down at a slight angle

back and thrusting the kicking hip forward. The body leans back to provide additional range as the kick descends.

Many martial artists use the kick to drive the opponent back and into range of a following technique but be prepared to react immediately your kicking foot touches down.

Axe kick can be used from close range as part of a combination technique. Begin by snap punching with your leading fist. Use the pull back of this technique to help thrust out a reverse punch. This technique takes body weight forward and off the rear leg. Swing the back leg around and up, dropping the heel on the opponent's head or collar bone.

Diagonal Axe Kick

Diagonal axe kick is performed in virtually the same way as the orthodox version. The kicking leg does not rise vertically; instead it swings up to either side and then it chops down at a slight angle.

13
The Circling Kicks

General Features of Kick

I have used the name 'circling kicks' to describe two techniques which both use the edge of the foot. The first uses the inside edge of the foot and the second, the outer edge. In both cases, the kick is a circling strike in which the foot is swept across the front of the body or face. The height of the technique is limited by hip flexibility.

The force generated by circling kicks is fairly considerable

The leg action used is known as 'circumduction' and power for it comes from the muscles of the lower torso. The force generated is fairly considerable because the entire leg is swung into the target. In fact the leg is almost fully extended, with only a slight bend at the knee.

The circling kicks are not the fastest of techniques but they benefit from the element of surprise in that they are seen less often than the other kicks.

The circling kicks are also used as blocks but more will be said about this later on.

Parts of Foot Used

Both versions of circling kick use the edge of the foot. Crescent kick uses the inside edge of the foot on the big toe side. Reverse crescent kick uses the outer edge of the foot on the little toe side. In both cases the big toe is lifted and the other toes are depressed as in side thrust kick. The ankle is fully flexed, so the ball of the foot faces vertically upwards.

Crescent Kick

Begin from a fighting stance by rotating your shoulders in the direction the kick is to take. The hips lag behind slightly, so a twisting stretch is set up in the muscles of the spine. As the hips begin to turn behind the shoulders, lift your rear foot and swing it around and forwards, with the big toe side of the foot leading.

The foot travels in an ascending arc, reaching a position of maximum height when it is directly in front of the body. The kick's momentum carries it on a short distance and rotates the

Begin from fighting stance

The back foot is swept up and forward

The foot travels in an ascending arc

Then it is swung back into the target

Momentum carries it on a little past the body

The spent kick is withdrawn in such a way that…

…it can be immediately re-used as a side kick

supporting foot. It is then braked to a stop and the flexed knee draws the foot close to the thigh of the supporting leg, from where it can be immediately thrust out again as a side kick.

The supporting leg remains bent throughout the kicking action, and providing you keep control over your centre of gravity, then there is no need to set the foot down immediately after the kick is withdrawn.

Reverse Crescent Kick

Reverse crescent kick is also practised from fighting stance. The back foot is swept up and forwards, diagonally across the front of the body to the correct height. The supporting leg turns outwards, as though for a front kick but instead the kicking foot is swung back into the target with the little toe side leading. The hips open out as the foot travels across the body. It is then braked to a stop and the spent kick withdrawn.

One-step Reverse Crescent Kick

This kick uses a step forward to accelerate the body. Begin from fighting stance and slide your back foot forwards, so it comes behind the leading leg. Adjust the length of your step to suit the distance to be closed. Swing your leg in an arc so it crosses the front of your body with the little toe side leading. Withdraw the spent kick before it travels too far, and set it down.

Spinning Reverse Crescent Kick

This more advanced technique closely resembles a 180° reverse roundhouse kick in the way it is performed. You can, however, distinguish it by the vertical attitude of the kicking foot.

Begin from fighting stance and step across with your front leg. Turn your head quickly so you can see the target. Raise the kicking leg from the ground and sweep it across the front of your body. Recover it in the usual manner.

Begin from fighting stance

Slide the back foot forward

Swing the kicking foot into the target

Begin from fighting stance

Step across with the front foot and turn your head

Raise your kicking foot and sweep it across the front of your body

Like all turning kicks, the success of this technique lies in maintaining smooth acceleration throughout. Any hesitation slows the kick and robs it of power. The novice student may find the spinning action a little unsettling but frequent practice will teach the spatial awareness needed to place yourself at any instant.

Faults to Watch Out For
The following faults commonly occur during practice of the circling kicks:

Body weight is biased, so a shift in the centre of gravity must take place before the kick can be launched.	Begin from a stance with a neutral weight bias.
The face and shoulders start forwards as the rear foot is lifted.	Relax the shoulders and upper body and control your centre of gravity.
The arms flap about during the kick.	Hold your arms firmly, yet in a relaxed way.
The foot does not rise high enough.	Work on your hip flexibility and strengthen the muscles associated with circumduction.
The kick travels too far, so it takes too long to recover.	The kick must not travel too far past the front of your own body.
The ball of the foot is not pointing directly upwards.	Configure the foot correctly through practice.

Training Aids
Use a mirror to check that:

- you are not jerking your face forwards as the kick begins,
- your arms do not flap about,
- your kick is reaching the correct height,
- your foot is configured correctly and travels across the front of your body,
- the kick is retrieved before it has gone too far.

A punch-bag is useful for:

- testing that you are developing sufficient power,
- teaching you how to absorb the recoil of impact.

Target mitts are excellent for improving accuracy.

Discussion
These kicks are derived from Northern Shaolin roots. They use both a long and a circling action which tends to make the user vulnerable to effective counter-punching. Because of this, they must be used with discretion.

They can be used to attack the side of the head without the radical body shifting required by roundhouse kick. Aim them slightly above the target, so they drop down onto it. When used in this particular way, they closely resemble diagonal axe kicks, though their main ballistic element remains horizontal, rather than vertical.

They can be used to sweep the opponent's guard aside, creating an opening for a second technique. This, however, requires accuracy because the blocking sweep is only the length of your foot.

14
Footsweeps and Hooks

General Features of Footsweeps and Hooks

Footsweeps and hooks are unbalancing techniques. They are applied to the opponent's ankles, shins or lower legs to make him lose his balance. Loss of balance may be total, i.e., the opponent falls to the floor, or momentary, in which case balance is lost only for a second or so. Loss of balance provokes an automatic series of reactions, during which the opponent is incapable of co-ordinated counter-attack.

Only a child who is learning to walk is aware of the complex muscular co-ordination needed just to stand upright. When the centre of gravity is moving, the margin for error is reduced. The footsweep and hook exploit this inherent instability by moving the opponent's foot, preferably as he is about to transfer weight on it.

The distinction between hook and footsweep is a fine one but for our purposes, a footsweep uses a jarring impact to literally knock the opponent's foot, whilst a hook uses a drawing out motion.

Parts of Foot Used

Various parts of the foot are used. The inside edge (on the big toe side) is used to scoop the opponent's foot. The ball of the foot strikes the opponent's shin, and the fully flexed ankle hooks behind his achilles tendon. The lower part of the calf and the instep are also used, the latter more usually in combination with kicks.

Footsweeps

There are various forms of footsweep, the most powerful being a rear leg sweep. Begin from a fighting stance and twist your shoulders in the same direction that the sweep will follow. This stretches the muscles in the spine, so they contract more strongly as the sweep begins. Lift your rear foot from the floor and swing it around, across the front of your body. Form your foot into the correct configuration and lift it no higher than necessary, so it skims over the floor surface to the target. Strike the opponent's ankle,

Lift your rear foot and swing it around

knocking it in the direction his foot is pointing, or to either side.

Maintain an effective guard and allow your supporting leg to swivel. Lean back slightly, keeping your face away from flailing arms.

Next practise a step-up sweep from fighting stance. Slide the back foot forwards while maintaining an effective guard. When distance is closed sufficiently, twist your hips and raise your kicking knee, pointing it at the opponent's lower leg. Thrust out the lower leg and slap the side of his leading shin with your instep. Turn your toes down and fully extend the sweeping foot. The action used is similar to that for a roundhouse kick.

This technique is less powerful than the rear leg sweep and works best when there is little weight on the opponent's front foot. It is also useful as a feint. Try the following combination. Face your opponent, with him in left fighting stance and you in right. Step up and foot sweep

to the outside of his front leg. He stiffens the foot, leaning out against the impact. Immediately withdraw your right foot and strike with your left foot-edge to the inside of his leading shin. The first sweep sets up the second and makes it more likely to succeed.

If your opponent takes up a high stance with feet fairly close together, then attack his front shin directly with the inside edge of your rear foot. A hefty impact is called for, so lean your upper body back slightly and project your hips into the sweep. By this means, the opponent's front leg is driven into the back leg, causing him to fall forward onto your punch.

If the opponent steps forward to attack, make a sideways evasion and seize his punch. Draw it out in the direction it was travelling and he will lurch forward. As he does so, strike into his shin with the inside edge of your foot.

A swinging, rear leg foot sweep is difficult to disguise and the opponent may simply lift his

Strike the opponent's ankle, both lifting it and knocking it to the side

Punch him while he is unbalanced

If the opponent uses a high stance, drive his front foot back

Step to the side and seize the opponent's outstretched arm

Punch him while he is unbalanced

Continue body rotation and sweep him with your other leg

Pull him forward off balance and...

...attack his leading shin with the edge of your foot

Jar him off balance...

...and use a reverse punch

Avoid the opponent's lunge

Slide your foot behind this leading leg

Perform a step-up roundhouse kick

Don't withdraw the foot completely

Jar him off balance

front leg, so your foot swings under it. Use this situation to your advantage by continuing body rotation, so your back turns towards him. Don't hesitate for an instant but set down the sweeping leg and pivot on it, extending the other leg and swinging it into the back of the opponent's supporting leg. If your action is fast enough, your second sweep will topple him before he has time to set down his front leg.

Reverse sweep need not involve a 180° turn of the body. Avoid the opponent's attack by stepping to the side. Slide your leading foot forward and behind the opponent's. An effective guard is essential at this point. Drive your heel down to the floor and straighten your knee, so your calf jars his leg forward.

Hooks

Hooks make use of your position to hook the opponent's leg in the direction it is facing.

Face your opponent from right fighting stance; he takes up left stance. Perform a step-up roundhouse kick to the side of his head using the instep of your right foot. Instead of drawing the

Drop your foot to the outside of his   Draw his leading foot in the direction it is facing   Punch him while he is unbalanced

kick back afterwards, let the foot fall to the floor to the outside of the opponent's leading leg. Then use a flexed ankle to draw his leg upwards and forwards.

If your foot falls to the inside of his leading leg, then seize his shoulder and pull him diagonally forwards while driving the calf of your forward leg to the inside of his knee.

Faults to Watch Out For

The following are common mistakes associated with footsweep and hooks:

Telegraphing your intention so the opponent can take defensive action.	Unless you intend to use the footsweep/hook as a feint, then disguise it with a reverse punch, roundhouse kick or such-like.
Pushing your face and shoulders forward as you attempt the sweep/hook.	Always lean back from a sweep/hook. An unbalanced opponent is sure to lash out.
Swinging your arms as you attempt the sweep/hook.	Hold your guard in a relaxed but firm manner.
Not using your hips behind the sweep, so the technique is weakened.	First twist your shoulders, then your hips behind a rear leg foot sweep.
Not configuring the foot properly.	Put your foot into the correct shape before making impact and judge range accurately.
Using sweeps/hooks when it is inappropriate to do so.	Unless you are much heavier than the opponent it is only possible to unbalance him as he is moving, or if he has a weak stance.
Missing with the sweep/hook and taking a long time to adopt a new fighting stance.	Be ready to follow-up in the event of failure. Either draw back your foot or continue through with the rotation. Don't stay in close, trading punches.

Training Aids

The best training aid for practising footsweep is undoubtedly an impact pad. Ask your partner to sit down and partly extend one leg. He holds the pad against his shin and you swing your foot around and into it, striking with the sole of your foot and using sufficient force to spin him around.

When you have mastered the technique, ask your opponent to take up a fighting stance and stand the impact pad on its edge to the outside, then later to the inside, of his leading foot. Practise footsweep against the pad, using enough force to jar him off balance. If the floor offers too much friction, then encourage your partner to use a stance where full weight is not loaded on the leading leg.

Use this practice to measure the recoil developed.

Chinese martial artists use the wooden dummy's leg in the same manner.

Chinese martial artists incorporate leg sweep techniques into their practice with the wooden man dummy

Discussion

It requires less effort (but regrettably more skill) to sweep an opponent as he is moving. Sweeping a moving opponent produces some of the most spectacular effects.

Look carefully at the opponent's stance.

- If it is too high, then sweep his front foot directly back into his rear foot.
- If it is too long, then hook his leg out forwards.
- If it is too wide, sweep his foot outwards.
- If it is too narrow, sweep his foot inwards or outwards.
- If he is moving, hold back until weight begins to settle on his front leg – then sweep it.
- If he is standing on one leg, then sweep it.
- If he is planted solid as a rock and in a stable stance, try another technique.

Only attack the lower part of the opponent's leg with foot sweep. In competition, a high sweep may earn an immediate penalty.

Many times the opponent falls unexpectedly and unless you are prepared to move in quickly, the opportunity is lost. Think about the direction in which he may fall. This too is important.

15
The Jumping Kicks

General Features of Jumping Kicks

The defining characteristic of a jumping kick is that when it strikes home, both feet are off the floor. This is what makes it different from a fast one-step kick, or a skip/kick. Jumping kicks rely upon explosive leg power to drive the body high into the air, and without this they cannot achieve their full potential. The hips must also be flexible and agility is needed to set the kick up.

Hardly less important is the need to know exactly where you are in relation to the opponent. With both feet on the ground this is not so difficult, but when spinning around in the air as part of a complicated movement, a whole new level of skill is needed. Moreover, all the parts of your body must be where you expect them to be, so they can be used in the correct way and at the correct time.

Parts of Feet Used

Jumping front kick uses the ball of foot, as does a version of jumping roundhouse kick; the other version uses the instep. Jumping side kick relies on the heel/edge of foot and jumping back kick strikes home with the heel. Jumping reverse roundhouse kick uses either the heel or the sole of the foot.

Jumping Front Kick

Begin from cat or fighting stance and jump high into the air. Depending upon the circumstances, you can either jump vertically upwards, or towards/away from the opponent. Obviously the closer to vertical that you jump, the higher the kick will be. Raise both knees and snap kick with the ball of the foot.

In order to qualify as a true jumping kick, the kick must be delivered whilst both feet are off the floor. Purists insist that the supporting leg should be raised high and not be allowed to trail. In practice, this does not increase force of impact and provided you are not trying to jump over an obstacle, there is no good reason to insist upon it.

Land on the balls of your feet with both knees slightly flexed. Quickly take up an effective guard, for one of the weaknesses of jumping kicks is in their landing.

Jumping Double Kick

This is similar to the jumping front kick described above except that two kicks are delivered whilst you are still in the air.

Flex your knees and jump high. Raise your left knee and snap kick hard. Immediately snap kick with the right leg whilst you are still airborne. Deliver the first kick as you are rising up and the action will help lift the body for the second kick. Keep your arms to your sides, land poised and take up an effective guard.

Jumping Roundhouse Kick

Begin from a fairly high fighting stance, bobbing down and then jumping vertically into the air. As you are rising, turn first your shoulders, then your hips in the direction that the kick is to travel. This twists the body so the foot can lash out horizontally into the target. Recover the spent kick by withdrawing the kicking knee close to your body and land poised, on the balls of your feet.

Begin from a fairly high fighting stance

Spring straight up, tucking your knees to your chest

Thrust the kicking leg out before the hips have fully turned

Jumping Side Kick (see next page)

This can be performed in two ways. The first is a straight up spring, with both knees lifted to the chest. Even as the body is still rising, twist in the air so one hip swings around. Thrust the kicking foot out before the hip has turned fully towards the target. Tuck the non-kicking leg up. Configure the foot so the outer edge leads. Gather the spent kick leg back in, and land on the balls of your feet.

The second method begins from back stance and uses a spring action from the rear leg to give a forward flight path. Turn in the air so the rear foot swings around, and thrust it out in a side kick configuration.

Jumping Back Kick

This is generally performed from a vertical jump or from a jump away from the opponent. Spring into the air and twist your body away from the target. Don't wait until you fully turn before thrusting out a back kick, with the heel leading and the kicking knee turned downwards. Gather yourself together quickly on landing.

Jumping Reverse Roundhouse Kick

This kick uses a spring, followed by a full 360° of body rotation whilst in the air. It is possible to twist only 180°, but this makes the technique less strong.

Spring up as before, lifting both knees close to your chest and spinning around in the air. Don't wait until you turn fully before extending your kicking leg with the heel leading the direction of rotation. If you allow the ball of your kicking foot to rise, the technique changes to a jumping reverse crescent kick.

Begin from fighting stance | Spring into the air and tuck your feet up | Begin to thrust out the kicking leg | Lock the kicking leg out straight

Jumping reverse roundhouse kick. Begin from a high fighting stance | Spring into the air and twist around . | Take your kicking foot out in a wide arc

Common Faults of Jumping Kick

Jumping kick needs a lot of leg power to get to the required height. Weak legs mean low kicks.	Use plyometric training methods to get the explosive power needed.
The supporting leg trails.	Pull both knees to your chest.
The kick is not completed when you land.	Kick as you are still rising, not when you have reached maximum height.
The kick is off target.	Learn where your body is in relation to the floor, and where your limbs are in relation to where they need to be.
Your arms flap about as you land.	Hold your guard in a relaxed but firm manner.
You land flat-footed.	Land on the balls of your feet and with both knees well bent.

Training Aids

Plyometric training is a must for successful jumping kicks. Practise single and double leg springs onto a high bench.

Use a mirror to check that:

- your arms do not flap about,
- your non-kicking foot does not trail too low,
- your guard is effective upon landing.

A supported punch-bag or large impact pad will tell you whether:

- you kicked high enough,

An impact pad will tell you if you have kicked high enough

● you kicked hard enough,

● you kicked accurately enough.

Discussion

Jumping kicks come from the Northern Shaolin group of martial arts. Legend has it that they were used to knock mounted warriors from their horses, but this would call for an extraordinary degree of skill. Straight-line flying kicks can accommodate little evasion on the part of the target and one wonders how many short-sighted martial artists missed their targets and flew straight over the horse's back!

These are the most spectacular of all kicks, and not the least effective. Practising them calls for good endurance and excellent timing. Used incorrectly, they give too much warning and provide the opponent with a golden opportunity to rush in as you land. They are seldom effective when used alone and are most often incorporated into a fast, close-range combination. The angle of jump can be adjusted to suit range. Use a feint to disguise the bob down.

Practise jumping kicks early on during a training session and use a well padded floor to avoid bruising the feet. The legs soon tire, so switch to practising another kick to give them time to recover.

16
Blocking Techniques Using the Feet

General Features of Blocking Technique

Kicking techniques can be used to deflect or prevent the opponent's attack. They work best against kicks; punches move too quickly to be deflected by a foot technique. Blocks which use the feet require a high degree of co-ordination and agility.

Pressing Blocks

These prevent an attack from developing by driving the edge of the foot downwards onto the attacker's kick. This prevents his knee from rising sufficiently to deliver an effective kick. It is important to apply the pressing block before the opponent's knee has time to rise to correct kicking height. The block must press down just above the knee rather than on the shin, and it may be necessary to close range before applying the block, so timing is of the essence.

Sweeping Blocks

Crescent or reverse crescent kicks can sweep the opponent's guard to one side, opening him to a follow-up technique. The first example which springs to mind is side thrust kick following a crescent kick.

These blocks require a high degree of accuracy to be effective since the blocking sweep is only the length of the foot.

Barring Block

The knee makes an effective block against kicks. Pull weight back over your rear leg and lift your front knee high as the opponent kicks. Turn into the kick so his shin or foot bangs into your knee.

The force of impact is lessened if you move into the kick by dragging forward the supporting leg. Most of a kick's power is developed at the end of the leg. Therefore the closer you move in towards the hip, the slower the limb is moving.

Sticking Foot Techniques

Sticking foot techniques are found in Wing Chun Kuen. These are used from extremely short range to deflect the opponent's kick. Because distance is so short, any attack needs only to travel a few centimetres, so an effective response must be nigh-on instantaneous. The best way of achieving this is actually to maintain physical contact with the attacker's foot.

In the first practice sequence, you have linked arms with your opponent and he raises his right foot as though to kick. You also raise your right foot and lightly press the inner side of your foot to his ankle. As you feel him beginning to move, thrust your foot forwards and down, so the heel of your foot strikes the knee of his supporting leg.

The second sequence begins from the same position except that your right foot is now outside his right ankle. Allow your knee to bend as his kick straightens, deflecting it outwards and past your body. As soon as it misses, thrust your foot down into the side of his knee.

The third sequence takes up from the opening position, with the inside of your right leg pressed to the inside of his. As he kicks, take his foot outwards and to the side, hooking your ankle under his heel. Then thrust directly back into his supporting knee.

Raise your right foot and lightly press it to the inside of his right ankle

Feel his kick begin with your right foot

Simultaneously deflect his kick and strike at his kneecap

Allow your knee to bend as his foot extends, deflecting the kick to the side

Let your knee bend as his foot extends

Then kick at his knee

Kick his supporting knee

Discussion

The sticking leg techniques are peculiar to Wing Chun Kuen and encapsulate the theories of that extremely effective short-range system. The blocking kicks work from a greater range and as I said, they require a high skill level. An exception is the knee-block. This punishing technique causes the opponent more damaged shins and toes than just about any other technique I know. Indeed, the effects of smashing your own foot into the opponent's knee can put you off kicking techniques for a long time afterwards.

17
Safe Training Hints

Don't train if you have a virus infection, because not only is it possible to infect your training partner(s), but you may also be at risk. Some viruses irritate the heart muscle and can cause problems during hard training.

A powerful kick can affect the heart even when no infection is present, so be careful when bracing impact pads against your chest. Female martial artists should always brace the impact pad against the upper arm.

Training intensity should be increased gradually. This is particularly important for students aged 40+. Young martial artists must not overdo flexibility training and should always combine this with strengthening exercises. Youngsters are also advised against trying to extend their limited anaerobic potential.

Training benefits asthmatics as long as they can distinguish between normal breathlessness and an attack. Diabetics can train normally too, provided that they keep some sugary lemonade on hand. Students with blood-clotting disease are advised not to train at all.

Some floor surfaces become slippery with sweat, posing a danger during high kicks, when the body is at its least stable. Do not train on an uncushioned, hard floor.

Do not repeatedly use unloaded full-power kicks, because these cause joint injury. Full power must only be used against an impact pad or punchbag. Train with a partner of the same size and weight, because a lighter partner will be unable to withstand your techniques.

If you have extensively used a punch-bag, your techniques will be powerful. Under such circumstances and in the heat of combat, your well-honed reflexes may produce a truly effective head shot. If this causes head injury, then your partner must withdraw from sparring activities for at least six weeks afterwards. A second blow to the head within that time will compound the brain damage already caused.

Repeated hard blows to the head may cause no obvious injury but eventually brain function is impaired and in serious cases, the martial artist becomes irreversibly 'punch drunk'.

If you enjoy non-contact competition, then train specifically for light impacts against target mitts.

I have heard it claimed that even an axe kick can be safely controlled but if so, there are few skilled enough to do this. The consequences of a misjudged but otherwise effective side stamping kick to the knee also bear thinking about.

Female martial artists should avoid impacts on their breasts. Various plastic shields are now available and provided a good fit is obtained, they offer effective protection. I advise against wearing a firm bra since this prevents otherwise unshielded breasts from moving away from impact.

A hard kick to the midsection can rupture the spleen and if this is not dealt with promptly, the consequences are serious. The kidneys are also easily damaged by hard impacts, but fortunately such damage is rarely fatal.

Male and female martial artists should buy a boxer's groinguard. This protects both the genitals and the perineum. Do not buy the type of protector that slips inside a jockstrap because this is shattered by kicks. It also tends to nip off any parts which all too easily stray outside the rim of the cup. If you can't buy a safe groin-guard, then my advice to men is to wear nothing beneath your training tunic. At least your genitals will be able to move out of the way.

Some schools allow full-power kicking to the thighs. The odd kick may do no lasting damage but repeated hard kicks can permanently and severely damage the muscle.

At one time or another, many martial artists believe that they have 'pulled their groin'. This causes a knife-like pain at the inside top of the thigh during stretching and high kicks. I used to think that the causes were tissue tearing as a result of high kicks following inadequate warm-up, or through ballistic stretching methods. I now realise that these are not the only causes.

Some schools teach a high roundhouse kick with the upper body both hinged and forward facing. This prevents the hips from rotating fully behind the kick and twists that part of the spine known as the sacro-iliac. If this is repeated, the joint can suffer injury, with symptoms very much like a 'pulled groin'.

Knee injury is the bane of kicking techniques and a high proportion of long-term martial artists suffer from it in one or both knees. It is commonly caused in one of two principal ways. The first is when the hips and upper body are rotating into a kick but the supporting foot is unable (through friction with the floor, for example) to pivot fully. The result is a tremendous twisting force that damages the ligaments. Once these are stretched, the bony parts of the joint are less well-located and damage to the cartilage follows.

The second cause is from repeatedly using unloaded, full-power kicks in which movement of the lower leg is braked by full extension of the knee joint. This too stretches ligaments and causes cartilage damage. The knee's ability to withstand unreasonable treatment may be curtailed through bad exercises which load the joint past 90° of flexion. These include fireman's lift from full squat position, bunny-hops and duck walking.

Prevention is always better than cure and I recommend using low stances during training, or as part of exercises. These increase strength in the muscles which reinforce the knee. However, once the knee has been damaged, the only recourse left open is to slow down the degenerative processes. Removal of the knee cartilage is not a guaranteed cure for the whole problem.

At the first onset of knee pain, review the way you are training and see whether it can be made less stressful.

In principle, it is always better to keep the knee mobile than to rest it for a long period. Muscles soon lose strength and joints stiffen up, so think twice before attempting to support it with strapping or crepe bandages. Work hard at strengthening the quadriceps muscles on the front of your thighs and avoid twisting actions and ballistic extension of the joint. This not only means being careful when kicking with the injured leg, but also when using it to support a kick delivered with the other leg.

Reduce training load when the knee problems flare up, but do not halt training totally for long.

Shins are also common injury sites and much pain can be avoided by wearing shin protectors.

At some time or other you will hurt your toe joints against someone's elbow or knee. Assuming that you haven't actually broken any bones, the following treatment will be useful:

- don't delay; get the swelling down with an ice pack. If you don't have an ice pack, use a packet of frozen peas;
- don't let the joint seize up – begin walking on it immediately in such a way as fully to flex the injured toe. This is extremely painful but it quickly restores mobility to the joint. Don't use bandages or strapping;
- try a contrast bath, alternately dunking your foot into adjacent bowls of hot and cold water. This is effective in bringing the bruise out.

Occasionally, one encounters a freak accident. There was a case in which two experienced martial artists were sparring and one's toe caught the other in his eye, causing a partial and permanent loss of vision. The injured party sued his partner for failing properly to control his kick. The incidence of such litigation is increasing and the moral is – don't practise unless you have a third party insurance indemnity. The cost of a policy is surprisingly little.

The Martial Arts Commission was set up in 1977 as a liaison body. It is an umbrella group of governing bodies concerned with making the practice of martial art safer and more rewarding for public and practitioners alike. I strongly recommend that you train only under an MAC approved coach.